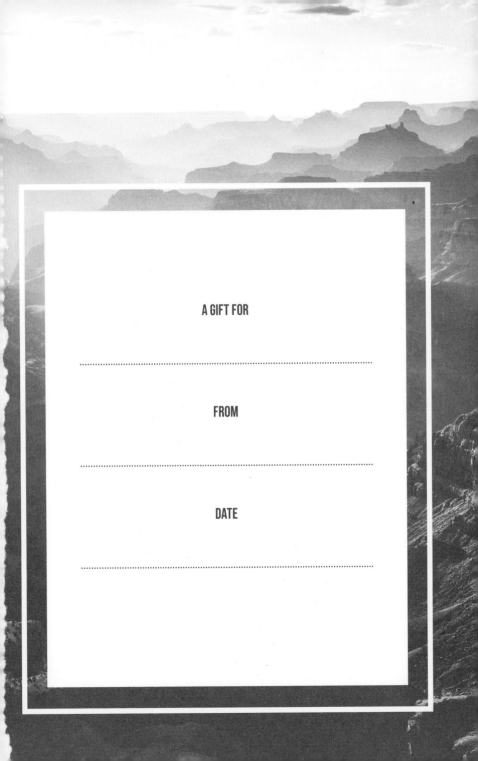

A GIFT FOR

....

FROM

....

DATE

....

ENCOURAGING
WORDS
for a
DISCOURAGING
WORLD

10 BIBLICAL PROMISES
TO BRING COMFORT IN CHAOS

DR. DAVID JEREMIAH

THOMAS NELSON
Since 1798

CONTENTS

INTRODUCTION

We live in a discouraging world.

That's a truth we've all experienced in certain seasons of our lives. No matter how many blessings we've received, no matter how buoyant our spirit, no matter how sturdy our faith, sometimes the darkness still seeps through. The weight of dejection and discouragement wraps around us like a shroud.

It happens to everyone—including me, including you. We see something terrible on the news, and it shakes us. We receive the phone call we've been dreading from the doctor, and it scares us. We don't receive a phone call from our loved ones, and it scares us.

Hope can be a fragile emotion, fleeting and frail. Cheerfulness and confidence are difficult to maintain in the face of trials. Discouragement, on the other hand, can come easily, even in the best of times.

How do we respond when we find ourselves in those starker seasons? By nature, we seek out sources of encouragement. The warmth of an embrace. The comfort of our favorite film or our favorite place. The levity of laughter.

Some people and some cultures seem to have a special talent for encouraging words. The Irish, for example, have developed a liturgy of blessings and prayers that are almost certain to bring about a smile on the gloomiest of days. Here are a few:

- "May love and laughter light your days and warm your heart and home. May good and faithful friends be yours wherever you may roam. May peace and plenty bless your world with joy that long endures. May all life's passing seasons bring the best to you and yours."
- "May your pockets be heavy and your heart be light. May good luck pursue you each morning and night."
- "May your troubles be less and your blessings be more. And nothing but happiness come through your door."

Talk about encouraging words!

But both now and throughout history, there is no greater source of encouragement in this discouraging world than the Bible. God's Word is a lamp to our feet and a light that illumines our path even when our hearts are dispirited and disillusioned—perhaps *especially* when our hearts are dispirited and disillusioned.

My goal for this book is to help you turn on that light by offering ten encouraging words from God's Word that will shine brightly even in the murkiest of moments. In each chapter we'll explore a specific passage of Scripture that is bursting with the hope that comes from God alone.

Are you feeling discouraged? These words are for you. Know someone who is feeling discouraged? These words are for them *and* for you. Think you might become discouraged sometime in the future? Then saturate yourself in these Scripture passages so you will be prepared to hold on to hope even in the most disappointing of times.

As you'll see in these pages, I've endured my fair share of discouragement. That's why I feel confident in the power of God's Word and convinced of the efficacy of these ten words. They are fountains of fortitude and springs of strength, and they are offered directly to you.

Don't miss this opportunity to soak in these waters and be encouraged again and again.

EVERYTHING

"His divine power has given us everything we
need for a godly life through our knowledge of him
who called us by his own glory and goodness."

2 PETER 1:3 NIV

W hat do you get for the person who has everything? It's an
age-old question, and one that has as many answers as there
are answerers.

In our modern world, however, we can at last find a little
clarity on this topic. Not from a wise person. Not from a library.
Not even from a gift-giving expert. No, if you type the question
"What do you get for the person who has everything?" into the

search bar on Amazon, you will receive a huge array of possible options.

One of those options is a solar-powered outdoor turtle statue with seven LED lights in the shape of succulents. Even the person who has everything probably doesn't have that! Another option is a pair of LED flashlight gloves for men. There's also a hot sauce–making kit. And an oversized blanket with sleeves that can be worn as a hoodie. And a T-shirt that reads, "I already have everything so they just got me this shirt."

I could go on, but there's just one more gift that caught my attention. It's a gag gift with this on the label: "It's Nothing!" Inside the carton is only air. That's right, for only $10.99 you can purchase the perfect gift for when you ask someone what they want for their birthday and they respond with, "Nothing."[1]

Maybe you think that's kind of a silly question. What are the odds any of us will ever come across someone who has everything?

Well, according to Scripture, those odds might be better than you anticipate. That's because God's Word identifies you and me and anyone who chooses to live as a disciple of Jesus Christ as people who have everything.

Feeling confused? Stay with me. In this chapter I want to share with you a specific Scripture from the writings of Simon Peter. I believe it will encourage you for the rest of your life. No matter what you face, this passage will strip away all your excuses for floundering and flailing. It will boost your confidence and enable you to make the most of each day, week, and year, whatever the weather of life.

You'll find it in 2 Peter 1:3–4. As you read this passage, don't skim over the verses. Listen to each word as if God were speaking just to you.

> His divine power has given us *everything we need* for a godly life through our knowledge of him who called us by his own glory and goodness. Through these he has given us his very great and precious promises, so that through them you may participate in the divine nature, having escaped the corruption in the world caused by evil desires. (NIV, emphasis added)

Because we live in a discouraging world, we often feel ill-equipped to handle the tough roads and difficult moments of life. When it feels like we're unprepared, we can easily be discouraged and distraught. We can also become isolated as we worry about others noticing (and even criticizing) our meager supplies.

That is never God's plan for us. Like a divine Outfitter, He wants to give us everything we need for the journey. He knows how to equip us to be people of character, able to face the ruggedness of the world with dignity and strength. He furnishes all we need for every condition. But we've got to turn

> Like a divine Outfitter, God wants to give us everything we need for the journey.

from our meager resources and embrace the abundant ones He provides.

According to Peter, who literally walked beside Jesus, you have been given everything you need for life and godliness. Not *some* things you need, not *many* things, not even *most* things, but *everything*. Believe it or not, God has already provided the resources you need to successfully navigate life with confidence and grace.

So what specifically are those resources? Peter lists several for our benefit in the first chapter of his second epistle—each and every one a source of genuine encouragement. Let's explore them together.

YOU HAVE GOD'S POWER

Have you ever experienced a spiritual power outage? For many, it's going to the doctor and hearing bad news. It's going to work and learning you've been laid off. It's answering the phone call that says your child is in trouble. It's watching the stock market plunge as you're about to retire. These things and more are bound to happen to you and me, for we have many troubles in this discouraging world.

That's why Peter began his second letter to the early church by telling us about God's almighty power. It's God's power that enables us to overcome the trials of life—to live the life for which we were created. If that feels big and inspiring, well . . . it is!

Verse 3 says, "His divine power has given us everything we need for a godly life through our knowledge of him who called us by his own glory and goodness" (NIV). What does it mean to live a godly life?

Godliness encompasses behaviors, words, and attitudes that reflect what God would do on earth if He were to come down as a person—as He did during the incarnation of Jesus Christ. A godly life manifests the purity and purpose of God from the inside out. It's literally a matter of Christ living His life through us consistently by means of the indwelling Holy Spirit.

Godliness may seem too lofty a goal to attempt. And it is—if we attempt it in our own power. But Peter was pointing us toward a power that will enable us to live a godly life: God's power. His equipping will supercharge our lives in a way that pushes through disappointment and lands us on the solid ground of encouragement.

Have you ever had the frustrating experience of charging your phone only to realize hours later that the cord wasn't plugged into the wall? It can be maddening—all that time wasted and still no power.

In a similar way, if you're not experiencing the power of God in your life, check your connections—you might not be plugged into the right energy source. God's endless energy and omnipotent power radiate from His Word. If you feel overwhelmed with life, immerse yourself in the Scriptures. Spend time with God in prayer. And let His power lift you, sustain you, and encourage you as He has promised.

> Let God's power lift you, sustain you, and encourage you as He has promised.

Think of all the energy radiating from all the stars in the night sky and ask yourself, *What source of power could so animate the universe? Where did all that energy come from?*

It comes from God. His power can light up the universe, fire up the stars, power the planets, move the oceans in their undulating tides, and give life to every creature on earth without being diminished by one kilowatt.

Since God has all the power in the universe at His command, He can do anything He chooses. And here is the incredible truth that should shake you to the core whenever you feel unequipped to handle what life throws at you: God has chosen to give you access to the greatness of His power.

The word *power* was in the vocabulary of nearly every Old and New Testament writer. If you go through the Scripture highlighting this word, you'll run out of yellow ink.

The Bible says, "Power belongs to God. . . . Yours, O LORD, is the greatness, the power and the glory, the victory and the majesty; for all that is in heaven and in earth is Yours" (Psalm 62:11; 1 Chronicles 29:11).

Consider Paul's prayer for the Ephesians: "[I pray] . . . that you may know . . . the exceeding greatness of His power toward us who believe, according to the working of His mighty power which He worked in Christ when He raised Him from the dead and seated Him at His right hand in the heavenly places" (Ephesians 1:18–20).

Paul used the word *dunamis* to refer to God's power toward

us, the word from which we get *dynamite*. Dynamite can do many things, but it can't raise the dead. But that's what the power of God did in the resurrection of Christ. And that's the power of God that resides in you.

YOU HAVE GOD'S PROMISES

In 2 Peter 1:4, Peter went on to tell us that God's power is communicated to us through His promises, and it's His promises that sustain our faith. Of course, we're not just talking about any old promises. These are God's "exceedingly great and precious promises."

What makes God's promises so great? First, they are incalculable.

No one can fully count the number of promises God placed in the Bible, although Dr. Everek R. Storms of Ontario decided to try.

"All my life," he said, "I have seen various figures quoted as to the number of promises in the Bible. The one most generally given is 30,000. Since this is a round number, I have always been a little suspicious about it. Furthermore, since there are only 31,101 verses in the Bible, it would mean that there would be practically one promise in every verse."

That inspired Dr. Storms to conduct his own study. According to Storms's calculations, there is a grand total of 8,810 promises in the Bible. About 85 percent of them are made by God to human beings. Only one book of the Bible contains no promise at all:

Somewhere in every single verse of the Bible, explicit or implicit, is a promise.

Titus. Isaiah contains more than one thousand promises. What section of Scripture most impressed Storms? "The most outstanding chapter as far as promises are concerned is Psalm 37," he wrote. "Practically every verse is a most wonderful promise."[2]

But with all due respect to Dr. Storms, it gets better. Many verses in the Bible may not be written in the form of a promise—and yet they are promises.

For example, think of 2 Corinthians 1:18, which says, "God is faithful." That isn't technically a promise; it's a statement of fact. But, oh, the promise implied by that truth! If God is faithful, then He will be faithful to you. You can read that as a promise!

The prayers of the Bible are implicit promises. When Jesus taught us to pray, "Give us this day our daily bread" (Matthew 6:11), He understood God can and will do that in answer to our sincere prayers.

Even the commands of the Bible are promises turned inside out. When Paul wrote, "Rejoice always," in 1 Thessalonians 5:16, he was issuing instruction, but only God can empower us to keep that command. You could paraphrase that verse to say, "Trust God, for He will enable you to rejoice in all situations."

So how in the world can you count the promises of God? You cannot! His promises are incalculable because the entire Bible is a virtual vault filled with infinite riches issued to you through every single verse. Somewhere in every single verse, explicit or implicit, is a promise.

Second, God's promises are infallible.

The Bible says, "For every one of God's promises is 'Yes' in [Christ]. Therefore, through him we also say 'Amen' to the glory of God" (2 Corinthians 1:20 CSB).

In other words, "Lord, have You promised to never leave us or forsake us and to work all things for our good?" He says, "Yes!" and we say, "Amen—so be it!"

"Have You promised to hear and answer our prayers? To watch over us and deliver us from evil? To give peace and strength as needed?" He says, "Yes!" and we say, "Amen!"

"Have You promised us an eternal home in heaven where sin, sickness, and sorrow can never intrude?" He says, "Yes!" and we say, "Amen!"

That equation works for all God's promises. For no matter how many promises God has made, they are all yes in Christ, and through us is the *amen* for the glory of God.[3]

Third, God's promises are available.

No matter how powerful something is, it's worthless if it isn't available. Without the endless treasure of God's promises available to us, we have no assurance about anything: no hope, no security, no safety, no encouragement, and no comfort. But God has given us His Word. His promises provide an endless supply of grace for us every day.

YOU HAVE GOD'S PURPOSE

Why does God provide you with His divine power through His promises? Because He wants to accomplish something in your life. He has a purpose in mind for you. Follow Peter's logic: "His divine power has given us everything we need for a godly life. . . . that through them you may participate in the divine nature, having escaped the corruption in the world caused by evil desires" (2 Peter 1:3–4 NIV).

> God has a purpose for you: to partake in His divine nature!

God has a purpose for you: to partake in His divine nature! That doesn't mean you're going to be God Himself. Only God is God, and living a godly life doesn't turn us into little gods. What it means is that His divine power transmitted through His precious promises can make you more like Him. He wants to infuse your personality with more of His joy, His patience, His wisdom, His influence, and His priorities.

He wants to give you everything!

At the same time, another process will occur in your life: You'll have a greater ability to say no to the corruption in the world that comes through evil desires. Because when you fill yourself with *everything* you need, you can empty yourself of anything you no longer wish to carry.

Imagine you draw a graph of your life based on this remarkable passage. The graph has two trend lines. The first line, hopefully ascending, plots your growth in godliness. The second line, hopefully descending, shows the opposite. We'll call it spiritual immaturity.

The more you lean on the power and promises of God throughout your life, the more these lines diverge. The godly line goes up, showing your increasing spiritual maturity. When it does, the ungodly line has to go down.

Put simply, your goal is this: more like Jesus, less like the world.

What could be more encouraging than that?

STUDY QUESTIONS

1. Read 2 Peter 1:3. What does Peter emphasize
   about the divine power of God?

....

....

....

....

....

....

....

....

....

....

2. Peter says that a godly life comes through the knowledge of God. How does this affect the way in which we pursue godliness?

....

....

....

....

....

....

....

....

....

....

....

3. When in your life have you struggled to have
   confidence in the divine power of God? How
   might knowing this verse change your feelings in
   future challenging times?

....

....

....

....

....

....

....

....

....

....

....

4. God urges us to be strengthened and encouraged by His promises. What would living life confident in the promises of God do for you?

....
....
....
....
....
....
....
....
....
....
....
....

5. Who is someone you know who models this "everything" life in Christ particularly well? How are they able to remain so close to Christ despite the stormy seasons of life?

....

....

....

....

....

....

....

....

....

....

....

6. How can you begin to live out the purpose of God for your life this week? Whom will you bring along to help you on this journey?

....

....

....

....

....

....

....

....

....

....

....

Dear Lord, help me to understand that in You I have everything. Teach me to be content in Your divine power, through which You have provided all godliness. I'm going to take hold of the saving knowledge of Your glory and goodness, knowing that it is the key to a fulfilled and content life in You. Help me to become more and more dependent on You as I trust in You. Remind me to always be connected to the power source that comes from a relationship with You, seeking out Your promises throughout Scripture and trusting that You will fulfill them as You have promised. Lead me to a greater appreciation of the purpose You have for my life, teaching me to partake in Your divine nature as You desire. Help me to take hold of Your power, promises, and purpose so I may be able to live the life You have called me to live. May I always live in Your grace as You strengthen me by the power of Your Holy Spirit. Lead me in Your love, because in You I have everything I will ever need. Amen.

2

SUFFICIENT

"And He said to me, 'My grace is sufficient
for you, for My strength is made perfect
in weakness.' Therefore most gladly I will
rather boast in my infirmities, that the
power of Christ may rest upon me."

2 CORINTHIANS 12:9

It was September 26, 1994, when I drove to Scripps Clinic for a full physical. A Monday morning that became a day I will never forget for as long as I live.

I didn't want to go to the doctor that day. I wanted to get some rest and recuperation after a Sunday slate of three services. My body was tired, my mind was tired, and even my spirit was

Everything
worthy in this
world comes
at a price.

in need of rest. Driving north along that familiar highway, I had no idea how much the peace and security of my life could be shaken. But the clock was ticking.

There's no need to describe all the details here. Just a few frightening phrases will do. "You have a mass in your abdomen that causes me some concern." "CAT scan." "Lymphoma."

I can't help marveling at the metaphor of my own journey to the doctor's office that Monday morning. I was on a familiar highway, my mind filled with plans and preparations for all the places I would need to go in the coming weeks and months. I was pointed straight and ready for a smooth ride. Full speed ahead. Little did I know about the bend in my road just over the horizon.

Somewhere along your own path, you've likely encountered your own bend in the road. Suddenly you faced circumstances you never expected or wished to encounter. I hope you've found it helpful, as I have, to read encouraging words from fellow strugglers.

Gordon MacDonald is a friend and fellow struggler. His fine book *The Life God Blesses* has ministered to me more richly than I can tell you. Gordon writes with wonderful insight about the methods God uses to bring blessings into the lives of His servants. In one chapter he coins a term to describe one of those tools. He calls them "disruptive moments." According to Gordon, disruptive moments are "those unanticipated events, most of which one would usually have chosen to avoid had it been possible."

He adds, "We don't like disruptive moments; they are too

often associated with pain and inconvenience, failure and humiliation. Not that they have to be, but that seems the way of the human condition."[1]

Few of us ever fully grasp that simple but painful biblical truth: the heat of suffering is a refiner's fire, purifying the gold of godly character and wisdom. Wouldn't we rather it be a simpler, more comfortable process? But we know life simply doesn't play out that way. Everything worthy in this world comes at a price.

Let's keep that in mind as we seek out encouragement in this discouraging world.

None of us enjoy suffering, but we can know one thing for certain: disruptive moments are occasions for comforting one another. For example, I cherish the hope that my own disruptive moments will enable me to comfort you in yours. Perhaps I can pass along some nuggets of wisdom that came at the price of suffering in my own life.

Pain draws me to God's Word, and in the midst of my trials, I've spent countless hours in deep personal reflection upon Scripture. One passage has been especially helpful for me in finding encouragement in the bends of life's road:

> And lest I should be exalted above measure by the abundance
> of the revelations, a thorn in the flesh was given to me, a messenger of Satan to buffet me, lest I be exalted above measure.
> Concerning this thing I pleaded with the Lord three times
> that it might depart from me. And He said to me, "My grace is

sufficient for you, for My strength is made perfect in weakness." Therefore most gladly I will rather boast in my infirmities, that the power of Christ may rest upon me. Therefore I take pleasure in infirmities, in reproaches, in needs, in persecutions, in distresses, for Christ's sake. For when I am weak, then I am strong. (2 Corinthians 12:7–10)

THE PURPOSE OF THE DISRUPTIVE MOMENT

"Lest I should be exalted above measure by the abundance of the revelations" (v. 7).

Paul clearly states that the purpose of his suffering was to protect him from the sin of pride. In the preceding verses, Paul described a time in the past when he had been granted an opportunity to be caught up into the very heavens with God. Now that's certainly a remarkable opportunity!

Such an experience had been granted to no other person, and Paul could easily have been filled with pride over his unique privilege. If Paul had a press agent, he would have most certainly billed Paul as the only man who had visited heaven and lived to tell about it.

But God uses disruptive moments to help us keep things in perspective.

THE PAIN OF THE DISRUPTIVE MOMENT

"A thorn in the flesh was given to me, a messenger of Satan to buffet me" (v. 7).

Scholars have spent untold hours speculating on the nature of Paul's problem. What was the affliction he was referring to? Some have suggested that Paul had developed eye problems, since we know that he began to dictate his letters to others. Another theory is that Paul was suffering from epileptic seizures. Sir William Ramsay even suggested that Paul had some recurring strain of malaria. You could fill a medical encyclopedia with other ideas that have been advanced: hysteria, hypochondria, gallstones, gout, rheumatism, sciatica, gastritis, leprosy, lice, deafness, dental infection, or remorse. Remorse? Don't forget that Paul had persecuted and tortured many Christians prior to his conversion.

Although we cannot be sure about Paul's "thorn," we can say this: The word used for "thorn" carries the literal meaning of *stake*. So what Paul wants to suggest to us is that he'd had a stake driven into his flesh—quite a disruptive moment, wouldn't you agree?

If we'd been told the exact nature of his affliction, this passage might have just seemed to be a story about Paul. We wouldn't be able to fill in the blank with our own personal afflictions, and our own "thorns" might seem outside the reach of God's grace. Instead, we're invited by 2 Corinthians 12:7–10 to identify with Paul's suffering. We're given the opportunity to realize that if God's grace was sufficient for him—whatever the nature of his suffering—it is sufficient for us as well.

> If God's grace was sufficient for the apostle Paul—whatever the nature of his suffering—it is sufficient for us as well.

Therefore, as strange as it sounds, we can find encouragement even in our most disruptive moments.

THE PROVISION IN THE DISRUPTIVE MOMENT

"My grace is sufficient for you, for My strength is made perfect in weakness" (v. 9).

There's the focus word for this chapter: *sufficient.* Without a doubt, being in a position of insufficiency is incredibly discouraging. Nobody likes to be burdened with "not enough." Not enough time. Not enough money. Not enough experience. Not enough strength.

The good news is we serve a God who has never been "not enough." Instead, He is always sufficient.

Paul didn't relish painful experiences any more than you or I do. In fact, he asked God three times to remove the thorn from his flesh. But God refused his request. He would not remove the thorn, but He would do something else. In the midst of the ordeal, He would give Paul all the grace he needed to continue his work. He also told Paul that His strength would be made perfect in this time of weakness.

Think of that: strength enshrined in weakness, power in pain. It completely defies and undermines the human approach to things—and that's why it glorifies God.

THE PRODUCT OF THE DISRUPTIVE MOMENT

"That the power of Christ may rest upon me. . . . For when I am weak, then I am strong" (vv. 9–10).

What God told Paul was merely this: "You won't lack the grace to do your job. You won't lack the strength to be My ambassador. But the creative difference will be this: Your weakness will serve to magnify the glory of My power in such a way that no one will ever again be able to explain your experience in human terms."

The weaker we are, the stronger His grace is revealed.

Or to put it another way: When "this little light of mine" becomes dimmer, His great floodlight shines all the more brightly.

THE PERSPECTIVE OF THE DISRUPTIVE MOMENT

"Therefore most gladly I will rather boast in my infirmities, that the power of Christ may rest upon me" (v. 9).

What a perspective! Paul sees himself in the midst of this disruptive moment and says, "I'm not the man I used to be. I've suffered, and I've felt my share of pain, yet now I find within myself an inner depth, a spiritual dynamic I've never known before. I've entered into the deepest mystery of life—the fellowship of Christ's sufferings. And now that I see the meaning of it all, I wouldn't trade a moment of misery for pure gold. In the end, you see, our pain offers us a far greater wealth. I've had a thorn in my flesh, and I claim it as a badge of honor."

So the apostle Paul has told us all about his weakness. Was he simply a passive person? Don't even consider it! The briefest study of his life demonstrates that there was nothing passive about Paul. This was the man who had scoured the countryside in search of Christians to intimidate. This was the man who had successfully debated the apostles on the question of Gentile salvation. This was the man who had faced stonings and beatings for the sake of the gospel.

Paul chose the most hostile settings in which to preach the gospel and plant churches. He scattered seeds of the gospel throughout Asia Minor and along the Aegean Sea. As the seeds grew, he trained the first pastors and elders in all the new churches. And then, in his spare time, he wrote half the New Testament!

> How can a man be both weak and strong? The answer lies in the phrase, "When I am weak, then I am strong."

So please don't call him passive. Paul was a mover and a shaker, a human dynamo. How, then, do we reconcile that with his claim to weakness? How can a man be both weak and strong?

The answer lies in the phrase, "When I am weak, then I am strong." That statement bears careful scrutiny. Listen well to Charles Stanley's eloquent paraphrase: "When I, Paul, in and of my own strength, am weak, then I, Paul, relying on the power of Christ in me, become strong, capable of whatever the Lord requires of me, full of energy and zeal to accomplish His will."[2]

Don't lose sight of this critical truth. As we've already seen, you will face discouragement in your life. You will travel your own bends in the road. You may even endure seasons when you feel too weak to go on, when you don't have the strength to make it through.

Even so, don't give up! Don't throw in the towel!

Why? Because God *does* have the strength, and His grace *is* sufficient for you.

Always.

Encouraging Words for a Discouraging World

STUDY QUESTIONS

1. Read 2 Corinthians 12:7–10. What phrase does Paul use to describe his unknown suffering? What does he say is the purpose of that suffering?

....

....

....

....

....

....

....

....

36

2. Paul's thorn in the flesh is emblematic of
   something we all face: "disruptive moments."
   How did Paul choose to respond to his disruptive
   moment?

   ....
   ....
   ....
   ....
   ....
   ....
   ....
   ....
   ....
   ....
   ....
   ....

3. What can we learn from the way Paul chooses
   to glorify God through his weakness? What
   weaknesses in your own life can be used to
   magnify the strength of God?

....

....

....

....

....

....

....

....

....

....

....

4. How can we live lives that admit our weaknesses, all to the glory of God? What would this do to shape an unbeliever's attitude toward God's sufficiency?

....

....

....

....

....

....

....

....

....

....

....

5. Knowing that pain draws us to God's Word,
   how can you begin the rhythm of running to
   God in your times of weakness and relying on
   His strength?

....

....

....

....

....

....

....

....

....

....

....

6. How can you take on the perspective of the disruptive moment this week and relish the opportunity to showcase God's strength in the midst of your shortcomings?

....

....

....

....

....

....

....

....

....

....

....

Heavenly Father, I am grateful for Your willingness to allow thorns in my life that lead me to depend on Your sufficient love more and more. Help me to appreciate the trials of this life as opportunities to grow in You and to be an example to others of a dependent servant of God. I thank You that You never leave me or forsake me in the midst of thorns in my life, and I have seen You be faithful in my life up to this point. I know You will continue to be faithful through all my life, and provide purpose for the suffering in my life. I pray that You will be near to me all my days, making Your strength known to all through my weaknesses. Help me trust that Your strength is sufficient for me at all times and in the midst of all suffering. May I lean into Your provision, having full confidence that You will continue to carry me as You have up to this point. Let my life be a reflection of Your light to all that may see, giving glory to You as the one who perfectly provides strength in all of my inadequacy. Amen.

3

BOUNTIFULLY

"I will sing to the LORD, because He
has dealt bountifully with me."
PSALM 13:6

Years ago, managers at a Houston airport noticed their customers had lodged many complaints about long waits at baggage claim. Their first solution was to hire more baggage handlers in order to make the loading and unloading process as efficient as possible. And it worked. The average wait time at each baggage claim was only eight minutes. Very fast for the industry. Yet the complaints persisted. People were still angry about waiting so long to receive their bags.

The managers then commissioned a study and realized the

wait times at their airport were within industry norms; their customers were waiting a normal amount of time. Still, the number of complaints alarmed them.

Looking into the issue more deeply, the airport managers realized it took most flyers only a single minute to walk from their gates to baggage claim. Once they arrived, they spent an average of seven minutes waiting for their bags. Those seven minutes seemed to be the root of the problem.

As an experiment, the managers arranged things so that passengers had to walk a longer distance between their gates and baggage claim. After the change, most people walked eight to ten minutes and found their bags waiting when they arrived.

The complaints stopped.

As one researcher noted: "Americans spend roughly thirty-seven billion hours each year waiting in line. The dominant cost of waiting is an emotional one: stress, boredom, that nagging sensation that one's life is slipping away. The last thing we want to do with our dwindling leisure time is squander it in stasis."[1]

Or, as the old song says, "The waiting is the hardest part."[2]

David knew much about the pain of waiting. He lived for almost ten years in the terrible tension between God's promise to make him king and Saul's desire to make him dead. David had killed a giant and become a hero—but he had to live the life of a fugitive. He was an anointed king—but he had to live like a beast of the fields. He was desperate.

Out of the pain in his heart, he cried out to the Lord. And

out of that furnace of his desperation came the incredible words of Psalm 13:

> How long, O LORD? Will You forget me forever?
> How long will You hide Your face from me?
> How long shall I take counsel in my soul,
> Having sorrow in my heart daily?
> How long will my enemy be exalted over me?
>
> Consider and hear me, O LORD my God;
> Enlighten my eyes,
> Lest I sleep the sleep of death;
> Lest my enemy say,
> "I have prevailed against him";
> Lest those who trouble me rejoice when I am moved.
>
> But I have trusted in Your mercy;
> My heart shall rejoice in Your salvation.
> I will sing to the LORD,
> Because He has dealt bountifully with me.

OUR STRUGGLE WHEN GOD DELAYS

On those occasions when you struggle with God's timing, it's good to know these feelings didn't originate with you. Not only did David express the feelings you've had, but he did so repeatedly. Read through the psalms, and you'll find a number of them

> So many of the psalms begin with a sigh and end with a song. But in life, you can't take in the song without letting out the sigh.

like the one we're exploring in this chapter. So many of them begin with a sigh and end with a song. But in life, you can't take in the song without letting out the sigh.

Just as a song has a refrain, this psalm's sigh has one—a recurring phrase that always comes back around. This time the chorus or refrain is repeated four times: "How long?" That's right, David was singing the blues. He was overwhelmed with a sense of the permanence of trouble. Trouble springs up when we want it least, seems to have no solution, seems to mock our most diligent efforts to lead a happy and peaceful life, and finally consumes our last ounce of patience. And David, much like you, finally lifts his eyes to heaven in exasperation and says, "How much longer, O God? How much longer?"

Aren't you grateful for the psalms that are such remarkable illustrations of honest prayer? I don't always pray with total honesty, and allow me to venture a guess that you don't either. Your friend at work brushes by you at the copy machine. "How's it going?" he asks with a smile. And you say, "I'm doing fine," or you might even say, "Couldn't be better."

But wait a minute! Didn't you have an argument with your spouse this morning? Didn't you just now catch a lecture from your boss? So you just told your friend a whopper, and you don't even think about it. How many times have you and I both done that?

Well, doing that causes damage to relationships with your friends because they have no idea what is really going on in your life. But we have much less success posturing before God. He is with you during the argument with your spouse. He is saddened by the confrontation with your boss. And when you force a smile into your prayers and say, "I couldn't be better, Lord!" He is again saddened. He knows what you're going through, and He has been looking forward to talking it over with you. He'd be much happier with an exasperated "How long, Lord?" than with your forced smile.

OUR SUPPLICATION WHEN GOD DELAYS

When God delays, we feel forgotten. We feel forsaken. We even feel frustrated with the Creator of the universe.

And that's okay.

Despite the desolation of his emotional state, at least David prayed. And what kind of prayer did he offer?

There is no textbook for genuine prayer. There is no professor who can teach it, no pastor who can make it happen for you. True prayer is a spontaneous outpouring of honesty and need from the soul's foundation. In calm times, we say a prayer. In desperate times, we truly pray.

> True prayer is a spontaneous outpouring of honesty and need from the soul's foundation.

"Lord," you cry, "I'm lost and helpless. I have nowhere else to turn." So having come to the end of your own limited resources, you are desperate enough to try your last resort: You go to the Creator of the universe, who loves you and made you and holds all the answers in His hands. That's when you pray.

David repeats one little word three times in his prayer of desperation: the word *lest*. This is the kind of small, inconspicuous word on which the entire meaning of a Scripture passage can hinge. *Lest* is a conditional word. First, David says, "Lest I sleep the sleep of death" (v. 3). David was so worn out physically and emotionally that he fully expected to die. He seemed to have come to the last page, and since the book of his life story was about to close, it seemed like an appropriate time to pray.

Not only did he fear his own death, but he also feared his own defeat. He said, "Lest my enemy say, 'I have prevailed against him'" (v. 4). David was certain that Saul would come out the winner. David was preparing to surrender as a prisoner, and it seemed like an appropriate time to pray.

Perhaps worst of all, David feared his own disgrace: "Lest those who trouble me rejoice when I am moved" (v. 4). Everyone in Israel knew David was being pursued by Saul. When the enemy caught him, David would be humiliated, a subject of mockery. And the terrible thought of that for one who had been promised a kingdom made it seem like an appropriate time to pray.

Three great fears moved David to his knees. Quite frankly, he was not motivated to pray because he was a godly man, although we know that he was a man after God's own heart. David prayed in Psalm 13 because he was desperate.

Through the years, I've often observed how God steers us into that emotional cul-de-sac. He likes to corral us into a corner where the only way out is up. We have nowhere else to turn, and that's when we get serious about praying.

That's why you don't have to beat yourself up when you feel discouraged. The same was true of David! Yet as we'll see below, David chose not to remain in that place of discouragement. He moved out of it, and so can you.

OUR SONG WHEN GOD DELAYS

You've probably already noticed the remarkable switch that takes place in verses 5–6 of David's psalm. The first two-thirds of that song are sorrowful, soul-crushing expressions of misery. Then, all of a sudden, a different tune bursts forth: "But I have trusted in Your mercy; my heart shall rejoice in Your salvation. I will sing to the LORD, because He has dealt bountifully with me."

The psalm turns from a lament to an expression of triumph. Why?

The short answer is that David received a renewed vision from God. He recalled, as the spirit of prayer took hold of him and God counseled his hurting soul, that nothing had changed about God. Our Lord is changeless. He had been mighty in the past, and that had not changed. He had been loving and full of blessing, and that had not changed. He had a plan for

We can't change the future until it arrives, but we can gain wisdom from the past.

David, and that had not changed either. David remembered these things, and he sang with joy.

Had David been delivered from his plight? No, but in his heart and mind he saw that blessed deliverance, and he claimed the promise of God. David, the future king, had such faith in the future that he spoke of it in the past tense.

Notice also that word *bountifully*. Isn't that a wonderful word? A terrific term?

If you want to stay healthy as a Christian, you need to go back and remember what God has done for you in the past. You need to polish the monuments to the great victories in your life. That's among the wonderful reasons for keeping a journal. David consulted the journal in his mind of his dealings with his Lord, and he realized, "[God] has dealt bountifully with me."

How often David must have, in his quieter moments, thought back to that tumultuous day in the field, that day when he tried on the king's armor and couldn't fit into it. He must have recalled the intimidating size and fearsome demeanor of that giant whom he faced with only a sling and five smooth stones. God had dealt bountifully with him then, and that was an understatement. David must have reviewed it often.

David took out that nine-foot-six-inch giant with a single shot and, in doing so, preserved Israel. There was no way to experience such a thing and not realize it was God's work.

David must have thought back even further to a time when God gave him incredible, superhuman strength and adrenaline to challenge wild animals that were threatening his flock of sheep. Why, a boy of his age couldn't have prevailed against a bear and a lion without God's presence. God clearly had a special purpose for him. A bountiful purpose.

And it was undeniable that there had been times when Saul had been closing in for the kill. The game seemed to be up. David was right in the very grasp of Saul and his sword, yet a miracle had always arrived.

We know from the psalms that David called upon his memory often to nurture and refresh his faith. When anxiety for the future built up—as it did time and again—David faced it with the testimony of the past. His life might not have been what he would have chosen, but it was a life that could never have lasted that long without God's intervention.

What a terrible danger it is for us to become trapped in the claustrophobia of the present during a crisis. That's our first impulse. The clear and present danger is so huge, so imposing, that it blocks our view behind us and ahead of us. We desperately need perspective. We can't change the future until it arrives, but we can gain wisdom from the past. It should hold for us an absolute conviction on the question of who God is and what He's done for us previously.

Make your list and check it twice. Just what has God done for you? You lost your job, and you thought the world would end. What did God do? Your marriage was in terrible trouble, or perhaps you even faced the devastation of a divorce. What did God do? How about when one of your children broke your heart? Do you remember God's love for you then? Make a detailed inventory of His faithfulness in your life, and you'll be surprised at the length of it.

Not just surprised either—you'll be deeply and lastingly encouraged.

Psalm 28:7 says it this way: "The LORD is my strength and my shield; my heart trusted in Him, and I am helped; therefore my heart greatly rejoices, and with my song I will praise Him."

Does it seem strange to you that Psalm 13, so filled with misery, builds to a final note of triumph, trust, and praise to the Almighty One? There's nothing strange about it. That's the way faith should work. We come to God honestly, pour our hearts out to Him, and experience renewed faith as He prods our memories and reaffirms His love.

Right now, today, you can smile even when surrounded by discouraging people in a discouraging world. Because God has dealt bountifully with you.

STUDY QUESTIONS

1. Take a moment to read Psalm 13. What is David's initial emotional state, and how does it change throughout the psalm?

....

....

....

....

....

....

....

....

....

2. What can we learn from David about the benefits of remembering God's past faithfulness in our present circumstances?

....
....
....
....
....
....
....
....
....
....
....
....

3. Why do we tend to give desirable answers about
   how we're doing as opposed to real ones? How
   has this affected your prayers in times of distress?

....

....

....

....

....

....

....

....

....

....

....

4. What monuments in your life do you have to showcase God's past faithfulness in dealing with you bountifully? How can you look to those monuments for encouragement?

....

....

....

....

....

....

....

....

....

....

....

....

5. What have you done so far to journal or record those monuments? What might this look like moving forward?

....

....

....

....

....

....

....

....

....

....

....

....

6. What can you do this week to begin praying
   more honest prayers about the things you're
   struggling with? Whom can you ask to join you?

....

....

....

....

....

....

....

....

....

....

....

....

God, give me the strength to be honest with You and to express my discontent in challenging situations. Help me to have an authentic relationship with You in which I confess to You what is troubling me and when I feel forgotten, forsaken, or frustrated with You. Continue to remind me of Your faithfulness as I trust in You, and teach me to depend on You more and more instead of pulling away from You in times of delay. May I always think of You first when I go through heartache and always be honest to tell You when I'm struggling with the fact that You have not yet intervened in the way I expected. Forgive me when I expect things to be resolved in my way and in my own timing, and help me to trust in Your perfect way and Your perfect timing. Let my life be a model of honesty and transparency for others to follow as they also pursue You, and help my genuine desire to grow closer to You be reflected in my prayers and the way in which I talk about my circumstances and the ways in which I am confident You will move for my good and Your glory. Amen.

4

REFUGE

"I cried out to You, O LORD:
I said, 'You are my refuge,
My portion in the land of the living.'"

PSALM 142:5

Like most people around the world, I spent much of June and July 2018 captivated by the story of the Chiang Rai Wild Boars of Thailand. I'm speaking of the twelve boys and their coach who spent two weeks trapped in the Tham Luang cave system, only to be rescued in dramatic fashion by an army of volunteers and divers from around the world.

If you remember, the boys and their soccer coach visited the caves after practice on a Saturday afternoon. They planned to spend an hour or so hiking through the caves with their flashlights. But heavy rains and rapid flooding cut off their exit and forced them deeper into the mountain.

It took a week for rescuers to find them in the labyrinthine tunnels. Amazingly, everyone was still alive—Coach Ake and all twelve boys. Families and friends rejoiced. Thai Navy SEALs brought food and other supplies to help the boys regain their strength. There was hope!

But how to escape? The caves were completely dark, the water was icy, and many places in the tunnel were so narrow that divers had to remove their air tanks before squeezing through. One experienced rescue worker had already died while navigating the complex tunnels. How could the coach and the boys—many of whom did not know how to swim—make a safe return to the outside world?

The answer was both daring and dangerous. Each boy was given a full-face air mask to ensure he could breathe somewhat normally, then he was clipped to a diver. Another diver assisted each primary rescuer. In small groups, all thirteen victims were slowly and carefully guided, pulled, dragged, and carried between their pocket of air inside the cave and its exit.

Do you remember the media coverage during those days? It was constant! And when word finally broke that all twelve boys and Coach Ake had been rescued successfully, it seemed like the whole world celebrated. What a moment![1]

When you think about it, a cave is a powerful metaphor for

discouragement and despair. Caves are places of darkness, tightness, and uncertainty. They often inspire fear and doubt. They can even be places of death.

It's interesting, then, that David wrote Psalm 142 while he was hiding in a cave. The headline before the psalm specifically labels it as "A Contemplation of David. A Prayer when he was in the cave."

Many of us have descended into the cold, darkened reaches of the cave of despair. That cave has its own twists and hidden passages, and we can feel lost. We begin to imagine God has forgotten us, that His comfort doesn't extend to these dark passages. Or perhaps we feel in our honest moments that He just doesn't care.

David confessed to us in Psalm 142:3 that his spirit within was "overwhelmed." The Hebrew words literally mean "the muffling of my spirit." What vivid terminology. Have you ever felt a muffled spirit? David had come to a place where he began to distrust his powers of judgment. He was no longer certain where to turn or what course to take. Life had become a great flood rushing in upon him, and he struggled to stand firm against the current.

David also felt deserted and alone. "For there is no one who acknowledges me; refuge has failed me; no one cares for my soul" (v. 4).

Problems tend to isolate us. I am the kind of individual who is certain to turn inward when the problems come. Like

There is never
a cave too dark
for God's light
to illuminate.

a turtle, my head snaps quietly back into my thick, protective shell. I want to sort it all out for myself without outside interference. I think that's true for most of us: We seek the nearest cave that might offer protection from the world and its questions.

Scripture commentator Alexander MacLaren offers this description of the process: "The soul that has to wade through deep waters has always to do it alone. . . . We have companions in joy, but sorrow we have to face by ourselves. . . . Unless we have Jesus with us in the darkness, we have no one."[2]

For these reasons and more, David declared, "I am brought very low" (Psalm 142:6).

Even so, David discovered (or perhaps remembered) what is true for all children of God: There is never a pit too deep to escape. There is never a cave too dark for God's light to illuminate, which is how David ultimately defeated his discouragement.

There in the cave of Adullam, David traveled a path to liberation from the imprisonment of his mind, and he left a map for all of us to follow when we, too, need encouragement.

DAVID VERBALIZED HIS PROBLEMS TO GOD

Have you ever asked the following questions? *Why should I tell God my problems? If He knows everything, why should I bother to go into all the details?*

All I have to offer you is the biblical answer to that question, and I believe it is sufficient for us. We tell God about our problems because He has commanded us to do so. That certainly seems reason enough for me; how about you?

Even so, I can think of a few other reasons to open up before God. One of these can be found at the beginning of this psalm. Let David spell it out for you—not once but three times:

- "I cry out to the LORD with my voice" (v. 1).
- "I cried out to You, O LORD" (v. 5).
- "Attend to my cry" (v. 6).

Perhaps David was a man after God's own heart because he was willing to share his own heart with God. He poured it all out before his Father, didn't he? When David felt he'd really love to see his enemies all die violently, that's exactly what he said. When he felt terribly sorry for himself, he shared exactly that. If you or I wrote a book of psalms, just how accurate a map of our souls would we lay out? Our map of the geography of David's heart, after thousands of years, is precise, even down to the smallest detail.

Prayer should be a time of no-holds-barred, straight-ahead communication with God. We cut to the root of the problem, and we're not afraid to name names. When that happens, we feel a tremendous sense of unburdening ourselves before the most intimate Friend imaginable. He is listening, He cares, He responds, and we can tell Him anything at all.

How could we not feel encouraged by such an incredible gift?

DAVID RECOGNIZED HIS PRESENCE BEFORE GOD

David wrote, "When my spirit was overwhelmed within me, then You knew my path" (v. 3). David verbalized his problems before God. He unrolled them as if they were a great scroll holding all the secrets of his mind and heart.

In the process, he made a startling realization: All this time he had been pouring out his heart, God was already at work with David on his discouragement. Every moment David felt overwhelmed by problems, God was busy dealing with them. Every second David despaired over the lack of God's presence, God was right there, as close as ever.

God knew about David and his depression and every single problem he'd ever had or would have in the future. God knows. Our term for that is *omniscient*. It means He knows every detail of your life and your feelings. Isn't that a comfort?

DAVID REALIZED HIS PROVISION IN GOD

He says, "You are my refuge, my portion in the land of the living" (v. 5).

There's the key word for this chapter: *refuge*. David remembered he was praying to the Creator of heaven and earth. He began to rejoice in the provision God had made for him. An old preacher once commented unforgettably on this verse: "There's no living in the land of the living like living in the living God!"

The land of the living is not a reference to eternity or heaven.

It is a reference to living right now. Aren't you glad the Bible has been written for people who are living in the land of the living? It's about so much more than "pie in the sky in the sweet by and by."

The Bible is written for the rough realities of life, the nitty-gritty of the here and now. It is intended to help those of us who rise every morning, drive to work, and punch the clock to face genuine challenges. Its pages are filled with real-life solutions for real-life problems.

> The Bible is written for the rough realities of life, the nitty-gritty of the here and now.

Therefore, we can find genuine encouragement in God's Word and God's words. They are a source of refuge.

DAVID RESUMED HIS PRAISE TO GOD

David wrote, "Bring my soul out of prison, that I may praise Your name; the righteous shall surround me, for You shall deal bountifully with me" (v. 7).

There's that word *bountifully* again, which was the theme of the previous chapter. David had moved from the depths to the heights in these few verses, and he was ready to praise God once more. Prayer will do that for us. We can pray our way right through the pressure. We can pray our way right through the sickness. We can pray our way right through the crises and the losses and the fears. If we will only come before Him honestly, He'll meet the needs in our lives—every one of them.

David traveled from prison to praise. He recorded the journey in his masterpiece known as Psalm 142. And I like to imagine that he wrote a sequel. I enjoy picturing him recording the final word of Psalm 142, then turning the page of his journal to begin Psalm 57—another psalm written in that same cave.

Read these words:

> Be merciful to me, O God, be merciful to me!
> For my soul trusts in You;
> And in the shadow of Your wings I will make my
>   refuge,
> Until these calamities have passed by.
> I will cry out to God Most High,
> To God who performs all things for me.
> He shall send from heaven and save me;
> He reproaches the one who would swallow me up.
> God shall send forth His mercy and His truth. . . .
> My heart is steadfast, O God, my heart is steadfast;
> I will sing and give praise.
> Awake, my glory!
> Awake, lute and harp!
> I will awaken the dawn.
> I will praise You, O Lord, among the peoples;
> I will sing to You among the nations.
> For Your mercy reaches unto the heavens,
> And Your truth unto the clouds.

Be exalted, O God, above the heavens;

Let Your glory be above all the earth.

PSALM 57:1–3, 7–11

In a cave of exile, David and his choir poured out their song of praise. Their concert hall was a natural geological sound chamber, one whose acoustics were designed by God long ago for this very earthshaking, despair-breaking moment.

The people sang on, praising God, their voices penetrating the massive stone of the natural ceiling to drift to the very portals of heaven, and perhaps even the angels stopped to listen. Can you hear it?

"Be exalted, O God, above the heavens" . . . our refuge.

STUDY QUESTIONS

1. Read through Psalm 142, paying special attention to how David was honest with God about his problems. How can David's transparency with God be an example to you?

....

....

....

....

....

....

....

....

....

....

2. As the psalm goes on, David turns his focus on God as the one who knows him. In what ways can you see the Lord's hand in your situation? Have you trusted Him to guide your path?

....
....
....
....
....
....
....
....
....
....
....

3. David does not take for granted the ways that God has been his portion and refuge; how does his focus on God enable him to withstand these trials?

....

....

....

....

....

....

....

....

....

....

....

4. How can you turn to God's deep care and love
   for you instead of focusing on the dark cave you
   feel trapped in?

....

....

....

....

....

....

....

....

....

....

....

5. What is God teaching you through the honest
   and vulnerable prayers of David, and how can
   you live this out in your own life this week?

   ....

   ....

   ....

   ....

   ....

   ....

   ....

   ....

   ....

   ....

   ....

   ....

6. Just as David turned back to praise, you can too. Meditate on Psalm 57 and pray this back to the Lord concerning your own need for refuge.

....

....

....

....

....

....

....

....

....

....

....

....

Heavenly Father, I know that You are good and that Your love endures forever. I thank You for this deep love because it sustains me. You know the trials I face and the difficulties that surround me. I ask for You to remind me that You are my refuge. When I become overwhelmed by the darkness that tries to harm me, please shield me. I know that You will not forsake me, because You are holy and perfect. It is overwhelming that You care for me. I praise You even when I am brought low because I know that You will not allow me to be destroyed. When I cry to You, I know You hear me. You will not allow the righteous to stumble. I ask that You help me to honor You in my trials, that my character would be pleasing to You. I give thanks to You for Your lovingkindness. I know that no matter how dark the cave is, You will be my light and my strength. You have seen my pain and have come to my aid. Please help me to see Your light and Your love. I thank you Lord, for You are my refuge and strength. Amen.

MIGHT

"Finally, my brethren, be strong in the
Lord and in the power of His might."

EPHESIANS 6:10

Canadian speed skater Denny Morrison won his first Olympic medal in 2006 and continued winning medals right through the 2014 Winter Olympics. After that, his eyes were firmly set on the 2018 Games in South Korea. But in May 2015 Morrison was in a horrific motorcycle accident and barely survived multiple serious injuries, including one that left him with a titanium rod in his leg.

As soon as possible he began the arduous process of rehabilitation and training, still determined to qualify for the 2018

Olympics. But the next year, after he and his girlfriend, Josie Spence, completed a three-week bike trip, Spence noticed suspicious behavior in Morrison: slurred speech, droopy face, left-side weakness, and a left-foot flip-flop that kept falling off. Spence knew the signs. She rushed Morrison to a hospital where he was diagnosed as having had a stroke.

Again Morrison recovered and dove back into training, now also struggling with the mental aftereffects of the stroke, including depression. Remarkably, in 2017 he and Spence, also a Canadian speed skater, both qualified to represent Canada at the 2018 Winter Olympics.

Training for that level of competition pushes athletes to their limits, but Morrison's teammates repeatedly said he was their inspiration to keep going no matter what. His coach called him the most resilient person he'd seen. And although Morrison didn't medal in 2018, his journey to get there was a victory in itself.

Describing his "grit" and determination, Morrison said, "When things stand in the way between you and what you want to achieve, it's that grit factor that gets you where you want to go. Goals don't come easy for anyone, no matter the line of work. But I think if you make a gritty attempt and push forward, you'll surprise yourself and everyone else with how far you can go."[1]

As Denny Morrison learned, strength comes in many forms. So does weakness. There's marital and moral weakness, financial and physical weakness, parental and job-related weakness. But the most debilitating weakness of all is weakness in your spiritual life—in your walk with God.

Suffering, challenges, and discouragements are universal. At some point, we all face something that shakes us to the core. The cause can be external, such as injury, loss, or mistreatment by others. It can be internal, such as self-doubt, poor choices, inflated pride, or addictions.

No matter what we may face, we need strength to face it well. Or, in the words of this chapter's key passage, we need *might*:

> Finally, my brethren, be strong in the Lord and in the power of His might. Put on the whole armor of God, that you may be able to stand against the wiles of the devil. For we do not wrestle against flesh and blood, but against principalities, against powers, against the rulers of the darkness of this age, against spiritual hosts of wickedness in the heavenly places. Therefore take up the whole armor of God, that you may be able to withstand in the evil day, and having done all, to stand. (Ephesians 6:10–13)

Maybe you don't feel strong right now. Maybe you know God is supposed to be your strength, yet within you there is weakness. What do you do? Just believing what the Bible says about the might and power of God doesn't overcome weakness. The apostle James reminds us that "even the demons believe—and tremble!" (James 2:19).

The great truth is this: You don't have to beg God for strength, and you don't have to look for strength. God is looking to *give* His strength to those who need it and will receive it!

Let me repeat that incredible truth: God has promised to *give* us His strength!

- "Have you not known? Have you not heard? The everlasting God, the LORD, the Creator of the ends of the earth, neither faints nor is weary. His understanding is unsearchable. *He gives power to the weak*, and to those who have no might He increases strength" (Isaiah 40:28–29, emphasis added).
- "Fear not, for I am with you; be not dismayed, for I am your God. *I will strengthen you*, yes, I will help you, I will uphold you with My righteous right hand" (Isaiah 41:10, emphasis added).

If you translate these promises from the Old Testament into the language of the New Testament, you hear the apostle Paul exulting, "I can do all things through Christ who strengthens me" (Philippians 4:13).

Now we're back to our earlier question: How do we get that strength? In a discouraging world, how do we fill ourselves with "the power of [God's] might"? What does that look like on a practical level?

Let's explore three ways we can access God's might.

WE DOWNLOAD GOD'S STRENGTH FROM HIS WORD

Biblical scholar R. A. Torrey was once approached by a man who complained he got nothing out of Bible study. "Read it," Torrey said.

The man replied, "I do read it."

"Read it some more," said the man of God. "Take one book and read it twelve times a day for a month." He suggested the discouraged Christian start with 2 Peter because it contains only three chapters.

Later the man said, "My wife and I read 2 Peter three or four times in the morning, two or three times at noon, and two or three times at dinner. Soon I was talking 2 Peter to everyone I met. It seemed as though the stars in the heavens were singing the story of 2 Peter. I read 2 Peter on my knees, marking passages with my colored pencils. Teardrops mingled with the colors, and I said to my wife, 'See how I have ruined this part of my Bible.'"

And his wife simply reminded him that as the pages of his Bible had gotten darker, his life had become lighter.[2]

That reminds me of something else I heard years ago: "If your Bible is falling apart, it usually means you are not."

The psalmist wrote, "My soul melts from heaviness; strengthen me according to Your word" (Psalm 119:28). But how do we open our hearts for God to do this?

Think of it this way: Your computer's hard drive contains all the applications you use for word processing, accounting, graphics, and more. When you launch one of those programs, the content of that application is "downloaded" from the hard drive into temporary memory where your computer's operating system finds it and delivers it to your computer's screen. Until that program is called on, it sits unused on the hard drive.

In other words, the program is just data waiting to solve a problem. You have to call on that data and apply it.

In a similar way, God's Word is filled with "great and precious promises" that "pertain to life and godliness" (2 Peter 1:3–4). All the strength we need for the challenges of life is found in the Bible. A Bible sitting on a shelf is full of strength-giving truth, but that truth changes nothing until it's moved from the shelf into your heart and mind.

> Like loving words from an encouraging friend, the words you find in the pages of Scripture will strengthen your soul with wisdom, joy, and light (Psalm 19:7-8).

We access the power of God by reading, memorizing, listening to, meditating on, and obeying the Bible. Like loving words from an encouraging friend, the words you find in the pages of Scripture will strengthen your soul with wisdom, joy, and light (Psalm 19:7–8). They'll impart the certainty of God's Word to give you strength.

WE DOWNLOAD GOD'S STRENGTH FROM WORSHIP

When your heart is caught up in the worship of God, something happens to you inwardly. Worship fills your heart with the worthiness of God and uplifts your spirit. That's why the Bible is filled with verses like these:

- "Be exalted, O LORD, in Your own strength! We will sing and praise Your power" (Psalm 21:13).
- "To You, O my Strength, I will sing praises; for God is my defense, my God of mercy" (Psalm 59:17).

One of my favorite Old Testament passages is from the book of Habakkuk. This book opens to us the heart of a prophet agonizing over God's inattention to his prayers. Habakkuk was watching his nation, Israel, fall into sin and rebellion. He couldn't understand why God didn't judge this nation, why God didn't even respond to his prayers. And then one day God answered Habakkuk and told him He planned to use the Chaldeans as the rod of judgment against the people of Israel.

At that time, the Chaldeans were the most wicked nation on the face of the earth. And yet God was going to use *them* to judge His chosen people?

The prophet Habakkuk was overwhelmed. Why would God do such a thing? It went against everything he'd come to know and love about God. When you read this short book, you feel the agonizing pain of the imponderable situation in which Habakkuk found himself.

The first words of the third and final chapter of Habakkuk read as follows: "A prayer of Habakkuk the prophet, on

Shigionoth" (3:1). While the exact meaning of *shigionoth* is not known, it is generally believed to be some sort of musical instruction. Hold that thought and look at the last words in the book: "To the Chief Musician. With my stringed instruments" (v. 19). Those two musical inscriptions tell us that everything written between them is a song. And it's one of the most profound worship songs in the entire Bible, concluding with these haunting lines:

> Though the fig tree may not blossom,
> Nor fruit be on the vines;
> Though the labor of the olive may fail,
> And the fields yield no food;
> Though the flock may be cut off from the fold,
> And there be no herd in the stalls—
> Yet I will rejoice in the LORD,
> I will joy in the God of my salvation.
> The LORD God is my strength;
> He will make my feet like deer's feet,
> And He will make me walk on my high hills.
>
> HABAKKUK 3:17-19

In the end, Habakkuk had to come to terms with this question: *Will I trust in the wisdom and goodness of God no matter what happens around me?* Instead of looking back or looking around, Habakkuk decided to look up. And his conclusion became this amazing hymn of praise.

How do we follow Habakkuk's example? We worship the Lord. We simply love, adore, and praise God's name—no matter what's going on around us. We know He will march with us to the farthest corners of the earth and to the end of the age.

As we worship, our life comes together in unexpected ways. And as we face challenges head-on, we keep praising and worshiping the God who is greater and stronger than any challenge in our path. We overcome our weakness with strength downloaded through worship.

WE DOWNLOAD GOD'S STRENGTH BY WAITING

We might not like the act of waiting, but the Bible says when we wait on the Lord, we will find the strength we need:

- "Wait on the LORD; be of good courage, and He shall strengthen your heart; wait, I say, on the LORD!" (Psalm 27:14).
- "Even the youths shall faint and be weary, and the young men shall utterly fall, but those who wait on the LORD shall renew their strength" (Isaiah 40:30–31).

The essence of waiting is to accept the unfolding of God's plan in His time. We're preparing ourselves to hear His still small voice when He knows we're ready. But waiting is the opposite of what our fast-paced world has taught us.

The first thing we need to do is slow down. Take a moment

God says the
way we gain
strength is by
retreating into
the quietness of
His presence and
waiting upon Him.

and consider how the frantic pace of our lives affects the peace of our souls. The Bible, by precept and personal illustration, points us in a different direction. To download strength from God, we need to make time to be with Him. We need to slow down, get quiet, and pray.

Isaiah said, "In quietness and confidence shall be your strength" (Isaiah 30:15).

Isaiah's word for "quiet" means ceasing activity, rather than the cessation of noise. This is the message of Isaiah 30—God wanted His people to stop their frantic activity by which they were trying to solve their own problems. The whole chapter is filled with the people's striving, running here and there trying to get help, and building alliances with pagan neighbors. You can feel the stress and tension escalating as you read the chapter.

As our challenges mount, our fatal tendency is to exert more strength and get busier. But God says the way we gain strength is by retreating into the quietness of His presence and waiting upon Him.

After we slow down, we need to get quiet. We're deluged daily with noise, distractions, technology, and the clamor of our culture. Sometimes in airports I'd like to sit quietly and read, but television monitors blare the news. In doctors' offices we have to put up with game shows shouting from the wall. In large cities the sounds of jackhammers, car horns, and sirens are unending. At home our televisions, laptops, tablets, and smartphones are constantly playing, beeping, and pinging alerts at us.

All that noise increases the tension inside us. It makes us feel weak. Uncertain. Discouraged.

If you want to strengthen your soul by attuning yourself to the voice of God through His Word and in prayer, learn to get quiet. In his time of greatest weakness, the prophet Elijah looked for God in the midst of a powerful wind, a great earthquake, and a flaming fire. But God's voice was not heard in any of those dramatic displays. It was only after the fireworks were over and the world got quiet that Elijah heard God's "still small voice"—the voice that gave him the strength and courage he needed (1 Kings 19:12).

WE DOWNLOAD GOD'S STRENGTH THROUGH WEAKNESS

As we saw in chapter 2, when the apostle Paul called out for God to remove his affliction, God answered him, saying, "My grace is sufficient for you, for My strength is made perfect in weakness." This assurance enabled Paul to declare, "Therefore I take pleasure in infirmities, in reproaches, in needs, in persecutions, in distresses, for Christ's sake. For when I am weak, then I am strong" (2 Corinthians 12:9–10).

At first glance Paul's declaration seems to be a contradiction. How can weakness make one strong? But Paul understood how difficult circumstances in his life taught him a profound truth about God's method for strengthening His children.

Years ago a TV commercial advertised a glue with the claim that when it repaired a broken object, the point of the repair would be stronger than any other part of the object. Under stress it would break anywhere else before breaking the bond of the glue.

That's what God did for Paul. He filled Paul's broken place with His own strength so that Paul was stronger in his weak place than anywhere else.

At the end of his life, in a Roman prison and abandoned by his friends, the great apostle Paul could still say with confidence, "But the Lord stood with me and *strengthened* me, so that the message might be preached fully through me, and that all the Gentiles might hear" (2 Timothy 4:17, emphasis added).

When you feel weak to the point of discouragement—or when you feel discouraged because of your weakness—remember that you are in the perfect position to access God's strength, God's might.

Because of who He is, you can take courage.

STUDY QUESTIONS

1. Read Ephesians 6:10–13. What does Paul say about the source of our strength? How does this fly in the face of our independent spirits and our tendency to try to be strong in our own strength?

....

....

....

....

....

....

....

....

....

2. What kinds of enemies does this passage say we will face? How does that reemphasize the need for godly strength beyond our own human strength?

....
....
....
....
....
....
....
....
....
....
....

3. How does the analogy of "downloading" our
   strength from God help us understand the way
   He infuses us with strength through His Word
   and our worship of Him?

....

....

....

....

....

....

....

....

....

....

....

4. Several passages of Scripture say we can draw strength by waiting on the Lord. How might this be difficult for us in our fast-paced world?

....

....

....

....

....

....

....

....

....

....

....

....

5. Why does the idea of waiting on the Lord when we need something seem backward? How can you begin seeking God in troubling times instead of trying to fix it by your own strength?

....

....

....

....

....

....

....

....

....

....

....

6. Which of the ways that God strengthens us do you need the most help with? (Word, worship, waiting, weakness.) How can you be praying this week that He will reveal Himself to you in that area?

....
....
....
....
....
....
....
....
....
....
....
....

Dear Lord, thank You for teaching me through Your Word that the power of Your might is sufficient to meet all my needs. Help me always remember the extent to which I need You and am lost without You. Restore my trust in You when it falters, and remind me of Your continued faithfulness to strengthen me as only You can do. Teach me what it means to be a dependent servant of the King, seeing each trying time as an opportunity to showcase Your might as the driving force of strength in my life. Help me to remain consistent in devotion to Your Word so that I may continue to be strengthened by it. Let my worship be poured out to You at all times and in all circumstances, and instill in me a sense of joy when I wait on You for strength. Remind me that it's in my moments of weakness that I am best prepared to be strengthened by You, knowing that Your power will be at work in my life during my weakest moments. Amen

6

PEACE

"Peace I leave with you, My peace I give to you;
not as the world gives do I give to you. Let not
your heart be troubled, neither let it be afraid."

JOHN 14:27

When Houston energy worker Shawn Baker was laid off in 2015, she opened a new business that quickly became a "smash hit." It's a place for angry, stressed-out, or anxiety-filled people to take out their frustrations on inanimate objects.

Inside the building are four rooms lined with thick plywood, all stocked with old furniture, dishes, burned-out TVs and appliances, out-of-date electronics, and even feather pillows Baker buys from junk dealers or used furniture shops. Customers get their choice of instrument: golf club, baseball bat, lead pipe, or sledgehammer. Then, after donning mandatory protective equipment, they close themselves in a room and smash everything in sight.

Baker named her business Tantrums LLC.

Customers pay $25 to $50 for five to fifteen minutes of demolition. After a session, the room looks like a war zone, filled with broken glass, feathers, ceramic shards, and electronic innards. People from all walks of life flock to Baker's business—mothers, businessmen, doctors, teachers, oil and gas workers, and even some therapists.

Customers rave about how beneficial a session of smashing has been, enabling them to relieve stress in a controlled environment. Baker said, "I would have never thought I would be helping people like that."[1]

It's easy to understand the impulse that drives customers to Shawn Baker's business. Anxiety is one of the defining symptoms of our times. According to the Anxiety and Depression Association of America, anxiety disorders affect forty million adults in the United States, or just over 19 percent of the population. It's a major factor affecting our general health; people with anxiety disorders go to doctors three to five times more than the general population.[2]

In a discouraging world, one critical source of encouragement is the ability to find peace.

Thankfully, Jesus Himself offers the gift to each of us,

including you and me: "Peace I leave with you, My peace I give to you; not as the world gives do I give to you. Let not your heart be troubled, neither let it be afraid" (John 14:27).

Jesus spoke these words to His disciples when He knew that in a matter of hours their lives would be shattered through His own terrible ordeal and death. Yet He told them they could have peace in the midst of trauma—an inward peace that brings confidence and stability.

The peace Jesus gives us is not a promise to remove the pain and stress of daily living. Those troubles are inevitable, and they will not be removed from us until the Lord comes again. The peace He offers is a calm, unafraid, unruffled confidence that, having placed our lives in His hands, all will be well. Nothing can harm our innermost being. Nothing can shake us from the intimate connection we've established with the Lord of the universe through our saving faith in Him. It's a peace we have despite external circumstances—a peace that cannot be destroyed.

> The peace Jesus offers is a calm, unafraid, unruffled confidence that, having placed our lives in His hands, all will be well.

How then can we find that peace? How do we receive it? Two central passages in the Bible give us positive, workable strategies to gain the peace we crave. They're found in Philippians 4 and Matthew 6. What are these strategies? We can reveal them by asking the five standard questions commonly posed by journalists: How? What? Who? Where? When?

HOW ARE YOU PRAYING?

Do you know the most often highlighted verses in the entire Bible today? According to Amazon's Kindle tracking, they are Paul's words about anxiety:[3]

> Be anxious for nothing, but in everything by prayer and supplication, with thanksgiving, let your requests be made known to God; and the peace of God, which surpasses all understanding, will guard your hearts and minds through Christ Jesus. (Philippians 4:6–7)

In this passage, the word *anxious* literally means to be pulled in two different directions.[4] It means to have a war, a battle going on in your spirit that's pulling you apart inside.

When we're under pressure, our tendency is to rush into His presence with our list of needs without even saying hello to the Lord. "God, I need this, this, this, this, and this. And I need it now and tomorrow and the next day. If You could go ahead and get it done ahead of time, that would be even better."

Sound familiar? Real prayer is a lifestyle of love for the Lord. Rushing into His presence with our laundry list of needs without pausing to truly focus on Him can depress us more than if we hadn't prayed at all! Have you ever started talking to God about your problems and found yourself more overwhelmed than when you started? It's because you're focusing on your problems instead of focusing on God!

A long time ago someone gave me a four-step outline for prayer that forms an acrostic spelling of the word ACTS: Adoration, Confession, Thanksgiving, Supplication. I recommend it to you as a simple way to order your prayers.

Here's something else I've learned about prayer: It is meant to be both preventative and proactive. We usually treat prayer as remedial, meaning we pray when we have a need or find ourselves in trouble. But in Luke 18:1, Jesus said that we "always ought to pray and not lose heart."

Proactive prayer is learning to pray in advance of hardship, asking for the strength to face challenges before they hit us. By praying in advance to overcome anxiety, you're preparing for the inevitable when your mind is clear and rational. Praying this way draws the power of the Holy Spirit into the picture, giving you future strength to overcome difficulty.

In other words, prayer shouldn't be your last thought; it should be your first thought—before you're overcome with doubt and fear. Before you're vulnerable.

This type of proactive prayer is an action we can take to rid ourselves of fear and fill ourselves with peace *before* we reach that bend in the road—that moment of discouragement.

WHAT ARE YOU THINKING?

We tend to think of peace and anxiety as emotions, and there's certainly reason for that. They are feelings we experience. However, we should not ignore the reality that our feelings are often connected to—and even produced by—our thoughts.

God desires
us to think
in ways that
reinforce
His peace.

Thoughts have power, which is exactly why God desires us to think in ways that reinforce His peace.

In Philippians 4 Paul wrote, "Whatever things are true, whatever things are noble, whatever things are just, whatever things are pure, whatever things are lovely, whatever things are of good report, if there is any virtue and if there is anything praiseworthy—meditate on these things" (v. 8).

With this list, Paul was telling us exactly and specifically what we are to think on, making it clear that we can and should direct our thoughts to what he describes. This is a command, an action statement. It is what we are to employ our minds in doing.

Our thought life is to be positive, uplifting, and redemptive because our thought life is the launching pad for our active, outward life. If you want your mind to be free of anxiety, make determined, definite choices as to what you allow into it. I cannot stress this enough. You are the guardian of your mind.

WHOM ARE YOU FOLLOWING?

To overcome anxiety and receive God's peace—the peace that passes all understanding—you can't just think about what is good, right, and true. You must also begin living it out. Often that means having a mentor who can show you the way. That's why Paul wrote to the Philippian church, "The things which you learned and received and heard and saw in me, these do, and the God of peace will be with you" (Philippians 4:9).

Paul's message to the Philippian believers was this: Take the lessons I've taught you and practice the things you've seen me do, and you, too, will begin to experience the presence of the God of peace.

If you battle anxiety, surround yourself with others who've learned how to trust the Lord when life is overwhelming. Spend time with people who understand the complexities of anxiety and the keys to success. Ask them questions. Study their lives. Listen to their stories. Learn from them.

WHERE ARE YOU LIVING?

We've seen the "how," "what," and "who." Now it's time to examine the "where" of finding peace. Where do your thoughts reside? Where are you living? There are only three possible answers: the past, the future, or the present.

Jesus said, "Therefore do not worry about tomorrow, for tomorrow will worry about its own things. Sufficient for the day is its own trouble" (Matthew 6:34).

Think about it. The past exists only as mere memory, and the future exists only in the imagination. Only the present exists as true reality. So why do we ruin the only moment of existence we have by pulling trouble from nonexistent places?

What's the point of borrowing discouragement from the future?

To experience peace each day, you trust God and receive His peace one day at a time. You won't sink under the burden if you limit yourself to taking on today's problems. But taking on tomorrow's agenda today puts you over the weight limit.

WHEN WILL YOU FIND PEACE?

Perhaps you remember the graphic photo of the "Napalm Girl" from the Vietnam War. It's a painful picture to see—a naked nine-year-old running down a dirty street, arms flapping, face twisted in horror. Other children are running with her, and behind them are billowing clouds of napalm wafting toward them and burning their skin.

The girl's name is Kim Phuc Phan Thi, and she was caught in a South Vietnamese bombing raid of a route used by Viet Cong rebels. The photographer who took that photo, Nick Ut, put down his camera (which he had instinctively picked up) and quickly transported her to a hospital, saving her life.

Kim endured decades of physical suffering. For many years she prayed to the gods of Cao Dai, her family's traditional religion, for healing. No answers came. Kim's dream was to become a doctor, and she actually began studies in that field. But the world knew her in a different way, and her government forced her to leave school to be available to speak and tour.

Devastated and desperate, seeking answers, she went to Saigon's central library and started pulling Vietnamese books of religion off the shelves, one by one. The stack in front of her contained a New Testament. After thumbing through several books, she opened the New Testament and began to read in the

Gospels. She was gripped by the sufferings of Christ as He bore our sins on the cross.

Shortly afterward, on Christmas Eve, 1982, Kim gave her life to Christ at a worship service. The message that day was about the Prince of Peace, Jesus Christ. Kim wrote:

> How desperately I needed peace. How ready I was for love and joy. I had so much hatred in my heart—so much bitterness. I wanted to let go of all my pain. I wanted to pursue life instead of holding fast to fantasies of death. I wanted this Jesus.
>
> So when the pastor finished speaking, I stood up, stepped out into the aisle, and made my way to the front of the sanctuary to say yes to Jesus Christ.
>
> And there, in a small church in Vietnam, mere miles from the street where my journey had begun amid the chaos of war—on the night before the world would celebrate the birth of the Messiah—I invited Jesus into my heart.
>
> When I woke up that Christmas morning, I experienced the kind of healing that can only come from God. I was finally at peace.[5]

Many years later Kim married and emigrated to Canada. She reconnected with the photographer, whom she calls Uncle Nick, and they talk every week. Today Kim's life purpose is to heal others through the love and peace of Christ.

Most remarkably, Kim ultimately forgave everyone who had

harmed her. She rose above her physical and emotional scars and made a choice to embrace the hope of salvation through forgiveness. She understood that unless she could forgive, she could not grow closer to Christ or bring others into His fold.

When will you find the peace of God? When you make the how, what, who, and where of His peace your priority. Look at how you are praying, what you are thinking, whom you are following, and where your thoughts are living. When you embrace these steps, then let our Lord fill your overcomer's heart with His peace.

How? Who? What? Where? When? You probably noticed we left out the question Why? As in, why is peace so often so hard to find? One answer, of course, is that we live in a discouraging world. We live in a world that pushes us away from peace because anxiety and fear are far more profitable.

Thankfully our Savior does not give as the world gives—neither does He take as the world takes. Instead, when we turn to Him, we can freely receive His gift of peace.

STUDY QUESTIONS

1. Read John 14:27. Jesus promises to His disciples that His peace is far greater than what the world has to offer. How can this peace transform your trials?

....
....
....
....
....
....
....
....
....
....

2. Having read Philippians 4:6–7, how can you
   pray with a consistent dependence on God as
   you give your burdens to Him?

....

....

....

....

....

....

....

....

....

....

....

....

3. Read Philippians 4:8. As you meditate over this verse, think about how your internal thoughts are affecting your beliefs. What steps could you take to be positive toward yourself, knowing that God desires you to meditate on things that are true, lovely, and good?

....

....

....

....

....

....

....

....

....

....

4. Anxiety and fear often come from a place of self-doubt or a lack of control. God has an answer to these issues. When we look to God as the One we are following, we no longer need control. Whom are you following, and what steps can you take to begin to follow after God?

....

....

....

....

....

....

....

....

....

....

5. Knowing that God desires for you to have peace,
   how can you live and abide in His peace?

....
....
....
....
....
....
....
....
....
....
....
....

6. Jesus can transform your life and heart with His peace. What burdens do you need to let go of so that God's peace can intervene in your life? Take a moment to use the ACTS acrostic to pray about that today.

....

....

....

....

....

....

....

....

....

....

....

Heavenly Father, my shield and my peace, today I come to You with the heaviness of my life.

Adoration: I praise You, for Your holy name is above every other name. You are my Creator and Friend. You are mighty to save and a peaceful God. You deserve all praise.

Confession: You know the inward parts of my heart. You see the sin and shame that I have. I confess these sins to You. I know that I need You in order to be holy. I ask you to forgive my failures.

Thanksgiving: I praise You that You have promised to restore me. Even though I have sinned and hurt You, You forgive me. I thank You that when I was dead in my sin, You gave Yourself as a ransom for my sins. I thank You for the blessings that I have seen today; You are my provider and my shield. You are my peace and my refuge. I thank You, knowing that I do not deserve these things on my own. You display such mighty love to me.

Supplication: You know the burdens I carry and the pain in my life. You know that these things have stolen my peace many times. I ask humbly before You, that You would intervene and that Your will would be done. Amen.

7

WISDOM

"Happy is the man who finds wisdom, and
the man who gains understanding."
PROVERBS 3:13

M any years ago I performed the wedding ceremony for two of the most remarkable young people I'd ever met. Bill and Rhonda were on the Navigators staff at Indiana University in Bloomington, Indiana. Their wedding turned out to be a church service. They both gave dynamic testimonies of their relationship with the Lord and of His leading in their lives. To this day, when I officiate at a wedding, I remember theirs.

About two years after their wedding, I received a call from Bill telling me they'd just learned Rhonda had advanced-stage leukemia. What a shock! We prayed together over the phone, and a few days later we got together to discuss the doctor's ominous prognosis.

For a brief time Rhonda went into remission. But within a few months her condition deteriorated again. Finally, she was admitted to Indiana University Medical Center in Indianapolis.

I'll never forget the afternoon I flew to Indianapolis to visit her. My heart was heavy as I walked into her room. But when I left the hospital, I had the distinct impression that I'd been ministered to that day. Rhonda spent most of our visit sharing with me what God had been teaching her through His Word, as well as some of the verses she and Bill had been memorizing together.

A few days after my visit, Rhonda went home to be with the Lord. In the hour before she died, she recited many of the passages of God's Word with which she had filled her life. According to the nurse who was with her when she died, "She went home to God in the middle of a verse."

What a way to die. Better yet, what a way to live! Being "filled with the knowledge of His will in all wisdom and spiritual understanding" (Colossians 1:9).

Living as we are in a discouraging world, we need a lot of resources to keep us not only encouraged as followers of Christ but effective as ambassadors for His kingdom. We've identified several of those resources in these pages: God's sufficiency, His bountiful grace, His might, and His peace.

Perhaps more than anything else, we need God's wisdom to navigate this discouraging world.

In one way or another, most of us have asked God for guidance and wisdom at some point. Does "Lord, help me know what to do?" sound familiar? You're not alone. Many pastors I know pray for wisdom as part of their daily routine.

If you sense that need in your life, as I do in mine, let's learn together how wonderfully open God is to dispensing His wisdom to those who seek Him.

Some years ago I was challenged to read through the book of Proverbs each month. Since there are thirty-one chapters in the book, reading a chapter each day took me through the entire collection of wise sayings twelve times that year. I've never regretted that time spent in Proverbs.

One of the early discoveries of my study was the many promises God has given to those who seek after and obtain His wisdom.

- "Happy is the man who finds wisdom, and the man who gains understanding" (Proverbs 3:13).
- "For wisdom is better than rubies, and all the things one may desire cannot be compared with her" (Proverbs 8:11).
- "When wisdom enters your heart, and knowledge is pleasant to your soul, discretion will preserve you; understanding will keep you" (Proverbs 2:10–11).

> Our ability to acquire God's wisdom is not so much a matter of doing as it is of being. It isn't so much an activity as it is an attitude.

Over and over Solomon said, "Get wisdom." The question is, how do we get it?

As I studied this question and read and reread the Word of God in search of the answer, I began to see some consistent patterns. Our ability to acquire God's wisdom is not so much a matter of doing as it is of being. It isn't so much an activity as it is an attitude—one we can develop together.

A HUMBLE SPIRIT

The first step in acquiring wisdom is a proper understanding of one's relationship to God. Solomon put it this way: "The fear of the LORD is the beginning of knowledge, but fools despise wisdom and instruction" (Proverbs 1:7). Job answered his own quest for wisdom with the same basic conclusion: "Behold, the fear of the LORD, that is wisdom" (Job 28:28).

What does it mean to fear the Lord? Does God really want us to tremble and quake in terror before Him?

Pastor and scholar Sinclair Ferguson describes the fear of God as "that indefinable mixture of reverence, fear, pleasure, joy and awe which fills our hearts when we realize who God is and what He has done for us."[1]

Another scholar wrote, "To fear Yahweh is to stand in a subservient position to him, to acknowledge one's dependence upon him."[2]

My interest in the subject of God's wisdom came at a time when I was making a major change in my own life and ministry. It was a humbling experience that caused me to depend on God in new and profound ways. After starting and pastoring a church for some twelve years, I sensed God leading me to a new assignment.

Each week, as I learned more about the challenge and responsibility of God's new calling in my life, I sensed a growing feeling of despair. The words of Paul described my attitude all too well: "Who is sufficient for these things?" (2 Corinthians 2:16).

When we are overwhelmed and confused in any area of life, the book of James says our task is to pray and ask God for guidance: "If any of you lacks wisdom, let him ask of God, who gives to all liberally and without reproach, and it will be given to him" (1:5).

And so I prayed for God's wisdom to calm my mind and clarify my path so that I might achieve His purpose. In a short time, that clarity came and confusion left me. My way was clear to me. You can imagine how encouraged I was to realize that my earlier fear and despair were merely stepping stones to the help I needed from God.

A person who is wise according to God's definition knows too well his own weaknesses. He never assumes infallibility. He who knows most knows how little he knows.[3] That's what it means to have a humble spirit, which is the first step in opening oneself to God's gift of wisdom.

Wisdom must be sought in order to be found; it doesn't arrive wrapped in a bow on the doorstep of your Christian life.

A HUNGRY SOUL

Wisdom must be sought in order to be found; it doesn't arrive wrapped in a bow on the doorstep of your Christian life.

A. W. Tozer made much of the hunger factor. He wrote, "The great people of the Bible and Christian history have had an insatiable hunger for God. He wants to be wanted. Too bad that with many of us He waits so long, so very long in vain."[4]

This is not just a modern problem. Five hundred years before Tozer, Lady Julian of Norwich asked, "God, of your goodness, give me yourself; for you are enough for me. If I ask for anything less I know I shall continue to want. Only in you I have everything."[5]

We have as much of God and His wisdom as we want to have. Our lack of wisdom is the result of our own lack of desire to know more of God and to know Him with all our heart. Do you seek to know God with all your heart?

In one psalm alone, Psalm 119, we're instructed to seek God with our whole heart six different times in six different phrasings. We're told to . . .

- keep God's testimonies with our whole heart (v. 2),
- seek God's commandments with our whole heart (v. 10),
- observe God's Word with our whole heart (v. 34),
- entreat God's favor with our whole heart (v. 58),
- keep God's precepts with our whole heart (v. 69), and
- cry out to God with our whole heart (v. 145).

If wholehearted seeking after God is a prerequisite for wisdom, many of us know where our problem lies: Our desire for God is too weak. If we want more of God, we must increase our hunger for Him.

A HEARING HEART

Only three months into his fourth term, President Franklin D. Roosevelt died of a massive cerebral hemorrhage. Vice President Harry Truman, with less than three months of executive office experience under his belt, was suddenly the president of the United States. Only after being sworn into office did Truman learn the shocking news: America was in possession of an atomic bomb. Secrecy about the bomb project had excluded the vice president from the need-to-know circle during his first three months in office. Ironically, he became the president to use the bomb later that year in Japan to bring an end to the war.

When Truman met with reporters the day after taking office, he told them, "I don't know whether you fellows ever had a load of hay fall on you, but when they told me yesterday [about the president's death], I felt like the moon, the stars, and the planets had fallen on me."

And a few days later, in his first address before a joint session of Congress, Truman expressed his dependence on God for wisdom in the face of his new responsibilities: "At this moment, I have a heart of prayer. As I have assumed my duties, I humbly pray to Almighty God in the words of King Solomon: 'Therefore give to Your servant an understanding heart to judge Your people, that I may discern between good and evil. For who is able to judge this great people of Yours?'"[6]

In 1 Kings 3:9 Solomon, in his unique supplication to God, asked for an understanding heart. The text literally says, "Give Your servant . . . a hearing heart" (AMP).

What a request! A hearing heart. Although we may have a humble spirit and a hungry soul, we still must learn to listen.

Once again we turn to Proverbs to learn the virtue of good listening:

- "A wise man will hear and increase learning, and a man of understanding will attain wise counsel, to understand a proverb and an enigma, the words of the wise and their riddles" (1:5–6).
- "Listen to counsel and receive instruction, that you may be wise in your latter days" (19:20).
- "Incline your ear and hear the words of the wise, and apply your heart to my knowledge; for it is a pleasant thing if you keep them within you; let them all be fixed upon your lips" (22:17–18).

There's so much of God's wisdom all around us, available to us from those who have walked with God before us. But we have to train ourselves to listen.

A HEEDING MIND

A humble spirit says, "I need God." A hungry soul says, "I desire God." A hearing heart says, "I will listen to God." And finally, a heeding mind says, "I will obey God."

To know that we need God is important. To reach out for Him is imperative. To hear what He has to say is crucial. But it's all meaningless unless we determine to do what He tells us.

We're not wise because we have God's Word. We're not wise because we desire God's Word. We're not even wise because we read God's Word. We're wise only when we keep and obey God's Word.

Are you looking for encouragement in a discouraging world? Obey God. That may sound strange, but try it even for a few days and tell me if you don't find exactly what you need.

STUDY QUESTIONS

1. Read Proverbs 3:13. In what ways does the wisdom of God encourage us in this discouraging world?

....

....

....

....

....

....

....

....

....

....

2. Reading through the various proverbs listed
   in this chapter, what pattern begins to emerge
   between true happiness and wisdom?

....
....
....
....
....
....
....
....
....
....
....
....
....

3. If gaining wisdom is more of an attitude than an activity, how can we cultivate hearts and minds that seek the Lord's wisdom in each moment of the day?

....

....

....

....

....

....

....

....

....

....

....

4. Knowing that godly wisdom begins with a
   humble spirit, what areas of your life need to be
   reexamined in order to be prepared to receive the
   wisdom of God?

....

....

....

....

....

....

....

....

....

....

....

5. Who is someone who has modeled well a hungry soul desperately seeking God's wisdom? What can you learn from the way they pursue God's wisdom?

....

....

....

....

....

....

....

....

....

....

....

6. Which of the keys for biblical wisdom do you
   struggle with the most? (A humble spirit, a
   hungry soul, a hearing heart, or a heeding mind.)
   How can you be praying for God to work in that
   area, and who can you ask to join you in prayer?

....

....

....

....

....

....

....

....

....

....

....

....

Dear Lord, thank You for Your perfect wisdom. I know that You desire to bless me through this wisdom. I pray that You would help me invite Your wisdom to mold my heart into one that honors You. You are holy and worthy of all of my praise and reverence. Thank you for allowing me to be dependent on you. Please help me to rely on You more, knowing that Your perfect wisdom will guide my steps. You are the only one that I need to be sustained. Help me to hunger for Your Word. Guide me toward a deep and all-encompassing desire to know You more. As I hunger after You, I know that Your Word promises to help give me discernment and wisdom. I long to hear from You in Your Word and to learn from Your wisdom. Help me to walk in humility as I learn from others who are striving after You. Give me an ear to hear Your guidance as I learn to discern Your will. I thank You for Your love and how You pour out Your wisdom through it. Amen.

8

COMPASSION

"But a certain Samaritan, as he journeyed,
came where he was. And when he
saw him, he had compassion."

LUKE 10:33

We're exploring ten words from God's Word that offer encouragement in our discouraging world. Now that you've made it this far into the book, I wonder if you've noticed a certain pattern in these pages.

Each of the words we've covered so far has highlighted how God delivers encouragement to us. At the same time, each of these words also reveals how we can live as sources of encouragement for others. It's a two-way street.

Because God deals bountifully with us, we can deal bountifully with others. Because God provides a refuge for us in times of disappointment, we can offer refuge to our loved ones or even to strangers. Because God is strong, we can bless others as conduits of His strength. Because God is wise, we can offer wisdom to help others extricate themselves from discouraging thoughts or difficult situations.

The benefits go both ways. Giving and receiving. Receiving and giving.

That pattern holds true for our next encouraging word: *compassion.*

I've relayed a lot of interesting stories in these pages. Some have come from history; others are from prose. But in all of human history and literature, no greater illustration of what it means to be compassionate exists than the story Jesus told about the Good Samaritan. This story, recorded only in Luke's Gospel, teaches us that we can never separate our relationship with God from our relationship with our fellow man.

Here it is:

And behold, a certain lawyer stood up and tested Him, saying, "Teacher, what shall I do to inherit eternal life?"

He said to him, "What is written in the law? What is your reading of it?"

So he answered and said, "'You shall love the LORD your God with all your heart, with all your soul, with all your strength, and with all your mind,' and 'your neighbor as yourself.'"

And He said to him, "You have answered rightly; do this and you will live."

But he, wanting to justify himself, said to Jesus, "And who is my neighbor?"

Then Jesus answered and said: "A certain man went down from Jerusalem to Jericho, and fell among thieves, who stripped him of his clothing, wounded him, and departed, leaving him half dead. Now by chance a certain priest came down that road. And when he saw him, he passed by on the other side. Likewise a Levite, when he arrived at the place, came and looked, and passed by on the other side. But a certain Samaritan, as he journeyed, came where he was. And when he saw him, he had compassion. So he went to him and bandaged his wounds, pouring on oil and wine; and he set him on his own animal, brought him to an inn, and took care of him. On the next day, when he departed, he took out two denarii, gave them to the innkeeper, and said to him, 'Take care of him; and whatever more you spend, when I come again, I will repay you.' So which of these three do you think was neighbor to him who fell among the thieves?"

And he said, "He who showed mercy on him."

Then Jesus said to him, "Go and do likewise." (Luke 10:25–37)

Here are four things we can learn about receiving God's compassion—and sharing it with others—as we engage this powerful parable.

COMPASSION CAN SURPRISE YOU

To fully understand the story of the Good Samaritan, you have to know that there were few people Jesus could have used as an example of compassion who would have shocked His listeners more—especially the "certain lawyer." The Samaritan was a foreigner with strange clothes and an odd accent.

More importantly, the Samaritans hated the Jews, and the Jews hated the Samaritans. This compassionate stranger wasn't like the others in the story, with whom the listeners could identify.

Out of all those who could have been neighbors to the injured man, the one who became a neighbor out of compassion was a despised foreigner, a Samaritan. This thought would have been particularly intolerable to the lawyer. Picture the moment when Jesus asked the lawyer at the end of the story which of the three men had demonstrated that he was a neighbor, and the lawyer said, "He who showed mercy on him" (v. 37). He could not even mention the fact that he was a Samaritan!

Like the Savior, the Samaritan brought himself near and made himself a neighbor. His actions in Jesus' story made his nationality forever synonymous with kindness and good works. When you drive through the cities of our land and pass the Good Samaritan Hospital, the Good Samaritan Clinic, the Good Samaritan Retirement Center, the Good Samaritan Church, you realize the reach of this New Testament story. Not only into our hearts but across millennia into our physical world, his compassion continues to be honored.

COMPASSION IS ABOUT WHAT YOU SEE

As you look again at Jesus' words, notice the priest, the Levite, and the Samaritan all *looked* at the traveler. But only the Good Samaritan *saw* him.

For Jesus, who is the ultimate Good Samaritan, compassion began with what He saw. On many occasions in the Gospels, Jesus' compassion was linked to seeing. In Matthew 9 He *saw* a crowd of people who were weary and confused, and He had compassion on them. In Matthew 14 Jesus *saw* another great multitude, and He healed their sick. In Mark 6 Jesus *saw* those who were like sheep without a shepherd, and He was moved with compassion to teach them.

When Jesus looked at those around Him, He saw opportunities to help. And in seeing, He was moved to compassion in many ways.

He was compassionate toward those who were lost spiritually; He was compassionate toward the sick; He was compassionate toward the needy; He was compassionate toward widows and mothers. He touched lepers, cured sick people, befriended social pariahs, and cherished children. His last acts were to pray for the forgiveness of His murderers and then to look beside Him and feel compassion for a dying thief whom He encouraged and assured of salvation. In His deepest hours of agony, never for a moment did

He take a break from showing compassion to others. The more difficult His life became, the more people crowded around Him with demands, and the closer He moved to a torturous death, the more loving, compassionate, and forgiving He became.[1]

May the same be true of you and me! Especially in this discouraging world, may we have eyes to truly *see* those in need of compassion and encouragement.

> Especially in this discouraging world, may we have eyes to truly see those in need of compassion and encouragement.

COMPASSION IS ABOUT WHAT YOU DO

When Jesus saw the brokenness of humanity, His heart was moved with compassion. And in this story, the Samaritan saw this broken traveler through the eyes of Jesus and had compassion for him. And seeing him, he had to do something.

If I have counted correctly, he performed nine different acts of compassion on this wounded stranger. Not only that, he did this at his peril. By getting involved in this situation and tarrying on the road, the Samaritan risked the same kind of treatment that had befallen the wounded man.

Genuine love always involves action. Unlike the priest, the Samaritan touched the traveler with hands of kindness and compassion. No ceremonial reason restrained him. He bandaged the stranger's wounds, bathed his sores, and helped him to a safe place where he could recover. This was true compassion on display. This was compassion at work.

"But whoever has this world's goods, and sees his brother

in need, and shuts up his heart from him, how does the love of God abide in him? My little children, let us not love in word or in tongue, but in deed and in truth" (1 John 3:17–18).

Isn't it interesting that the people at whom we frequently direct respect and kindness in our culture are often different from the special people to whom God shows kindness? God emphasizes the importance of those whom we would consider to be "down-and-out." When God exhibits His kindness, He never seeks anything in return. It's a pure act of love on His part.

That's good news for you and me because there are always bends in the road ahead. No matter how well things are going now, we will endure seasons of discouragement—which means we will be directly in line for God's compassion.

So we can be encouraged!

COMPASSION IS ABOUT HOW YOU DO IT

When Jesus asked the lawyer at the end of the story which of the three men had demonstrated that he was a neighbor, the lawyer said, "He who showed mercy."

That's what the Samaritan did! He showed mercy on this needy traveler. He cleansed his wounds with wine. (At that time, the alcohol content of the wine was often used to cauterize wounds and cleanse them.) Then the Samaritan poured oil on his wounds and bound them with bandages so they could begin to heal. He delivered his compassion to this man with great mercy and care.

True compassion doesn't weigh the cost first; it simply responds to human suffering with loving-kindness.

In one of the key New Testament verses on the subject of compassion, we're instructed about the manner in which compassion is to be given: "Having compassion for one another; love as brothers, be tenderhearted, be courteous" (1 Peter 3:8).

When I started at the church where I now pastor, I was going through some very difficult times. There was a lot of turmoil in the church. Being new, I didn't know other men in the ministry. One day I got a call from the pastor of another local church who said, "Hey, I know a little about what you're going through. I don't need any of the details. I just want to say hang in there. And I want you to know that I'm here if you need a friend."

Even more amazing, a few days later he was getting ready to go on vacation, and he called again. He explained that he was heading out of town and gave me his number. "I just wanted you to have my number in case you need me."

Talk about encouragement!

It's hard to express what this meant to me at that time. That simple act of genuine compassion lifted me up, renewed my strength, and let me know I wasn't alone. I've never forgotten it.

COMPASSION IS ABOUT WHAT IT COSTS YOU

I wouldn't be correctly expounding on Jesus' story if I didn't mention the cost paid by the Good Samaritan. Make no mistake, our compassion will also require us to pay a price.

Sometimes compassion costs us time; sometimes it costs us

more. But true compassion doesn't weigh the cost first; it simply responds to human suffering with loving-kindness.

At the beginning of the story, the lawyer asked Jesus, "Who is my neighbor?" (Luke 10:29). At the end of the story, Jesus asked the lawyer who was neighbor to the wounded man.

The conversation turned from "Who is my neighbor?" to "Who is neighbor to him?" In other words, the key question at the end of the story, and the key element of compassion, is not "Who is going to help me?" but "Whom am I going to help?"

And then the Master said, "Go and do likewise" (v. 37).

There it is. There is our command: to be compassionate, to give of ourselves, and to emulate the stranger in the foreign land who cared more than the temple priests and administrators, who cared more than the theologian who discoursed but did not act.

When you need compassion or when you need encouragement, remember this command. Yes, you should seek what you need from God. Yes, you should accept goodness and kindness from those who love you—even from strangers. But don't forget to go and do likewise.

STUDY QUESTIONS

1. Read Luke 10:25–37. If you were already familiar with this parable, what stuck out to you this time that you had not noticed before? How can this new insight help you better understand godly compassion?

....

....

....

....

....

....

....

....

....

2. How does the compassion God has shown us help us be more compassionate to others?

....

....

....

....

....

....

....

....

....

....

....

....

....

3. How did what Jesus saw affect where He was compassionate? How can we learn to have eyes for the people around us who need the compassion of Jesus?

....

....

....

....

....

....

....

....

....

....

....

....

4. Read 1 John 3:17–18. How does John emphasize the connection between seeing a need and acting on it? What opportunity for compassion have you seen recently that you can now act on?

....

....

....

....

....

....

....

....

....

....

....

....

5. How might a serious commitment to compassion cost you? What can you do now to prepare your heart for this?

....

....

....

....

....

....

....

....

....

....

....

....

6. What specific aspect of God's compassion on
   your life inspires you the most as you go out into
   the world seeking to share the compassion of
   Christ with others?

....

....

....

....

....

....

....

....

....

....

....

Heavenly Father, help me to be full of Your compassion as I seek to live a life that reflects Your wonderful character and magnifies Your marvelous name. I confess that I have not always played the role of the Good Samaritan in this parable, but I want to live out Your plan for my life and leave behind past failures. I am deeply grateful for all the compassion You have shown me up to this point in my life, and I want to in turn share this with those around me. I know You have blessed me so that I may be a blessing to others, including in the area of compassion. I ask that You would help remind me of my own lost condition without Your saving work so that I may grow in compassion for those around me. Keep me from the temptations in life to be like the several people in this parable who passed by before the Good Samaritan arrived, and help me instead to have his compassion. Let my life be clearly grateful for Your compassion and full of it for others. Help me to live like You in all that I do. Amen.

9

JOY

"The generous soul will be made rich, and he
who waters will also be watered himself."

PROVERBS 11:25

In the comedy *Cool Runnings*, John Candy plays a former American gold medalist bobsledder who's coaching the first Jamaican bobsled team to go to the Olympics. The bobsledders grow to like the American coach, and eventually Candy's character admits to a dark history. In an Olympics following his gold-medal performance, he added weights to the U.S. sled to make it go downhill faster. He got caught, disgracing himself and his team.

One of the Jamaican bobsledders couldn't understand why anyone who'd already won a gold medal would cheat. He asked his coach to explain.

"I had to win," said Candy's character. "I learned something. If you are not happy without a gold medal, you won't be happy with it."[1]

There's truth in those words. How many people have chased after money or power or fame or relationships or thrills or any other commodity because they believed once they had it—once they reached that pinnacle or achieved that goal—they would finally be happy. It doesn't work.

Strange as it may sound, our constant pursuit of happiness in America and throughout the West is one of the reasons we live in such a discouraging world. We are constantly trying to settle for happiness when we should be seeking joy.

"We Americans are obsessed with being happy," says theologian and philosopher J. P. Moreland. "But we are also terribly confused about what happiness is. As a result, we seldom find a happiness that lasts. But because 'the pursuit of happiness' is promised to us as a right in the founding document of our nation, the Declaration of Independence, we carry a sense of entitlement. We think we deserve happiness. And if we don't find what we consider to be happiness, we are likely to develop what . . . Alexis de Tocqueville called 'a strange melancholy in the midst of abundance.'"[2]

What an apt description of the attitude of most Americans. We are surrounded by all the things we think will make us happy, yet we are restless and dissatisfied inside.

The good news is that biblical joy isn't the same thing as

the general happiness that so often eludes us. Happiness is about what happens to us, and to an extent, it's dependent on our circumstances, our behaviors, and our attitudes. But the joy of Christ is much, much bigger. The joy of Christ is about a relationship with a Person. It's something we have access to, and it's something we are able to choose.

Therefore, be encouraged! As a follower of Jesus, you have the gift of joy. In fact, the Christian life is filled with notable milestones, and we can find joy in every one of them.

> As a follower of Jesus, you have the gift of joy.

THE JOY OF SALVATION

The moment of salvation is inexpressibly joyous. This is our eternal, spiritual delivery from separation from God and our entry into the kingdom of God. Jesus came so that we might be saved, and the New Testament testifies that this experience is an occasion for joy—for those converted and for those involved in the process.

Many tears of joy have been shed when someone estranged from God, or who has been an enemy of God, has become His adopted son or daughter.

In Luke 15 Jesus told three stories of precious things that are lost and then found, and each is an occasion for joy: the shepherd who left ninety-nine sheep to search for and find one lost lamb; the woman who lost a valuable coin and found it; and the prodigal son who was lost but found his way home. In each story Jesus spoke of the rejoicing that surrounds the saving of one soul, and He described the joy that results: "I say to you that likewise there will be more joy in heaven over one sinner who repents than over ninety-nine just persons who need no repentance" (v. 7).

After the Ethiopian eunuch was saved, "he went on his way rejoicing" (Acts 8:39). Luke recorded that the conversion of the Gentiles "caused great joy to all the brethren" (Acts 15:3). The Philippian jailer and his family were filled with joy when they became believers in God (Acts 16:34).

Never doubt that salvation, the most profound of new beginnings, is also infused with joy beyond description.

THE JOY OF BAPTISM

Ask most Christians which is the most joyful event in a church service, and many will say baptism. Joy surrounds baptism.

Years ago, when I was a pastor in Indiana, I became friends with another pastor who told me amazing stories of God's work in his congregation. One Sunday, as he was preaching, a homeless man came into his church and sat down in the front. He listened to the gospel message intently, and at the end of the service, he gave his heart to the Lord.

This church practiced immediate baptism. If you became a Christian, they baptized you that same day at the close of the service. According to my friend, this man was so joyful about his conversion and baptism that he came up out of the water, threw both hands in the air, and shouted, "Hot dog! Hot dog!"

He hadn't learned to say, "Amen," "Praise the Lord," or "Hallelujah." All he knew was "Hot dog! Hot dog!" My friend said that was one of the most joyous days he could remember as a pastor.

You can also find encouragement in the ritual of baptism— both yours and others. Each time that you get to witness another person publicly declaring their inclusion in God's kingdom is a reminder not only of the heavenly celebration taking place at that moment but also of the eternal jubilee still to come.

THE JOY OF TRIALS AND DISCOURAGEMENT

Yes, you read that correctly: You can find joy (and encouragement) even in moments of suffering and discouragement. Christian joy shows up not only in the happy times but also in times of trial.

Jesus' joy survived troubles and even flourished in the midst of them. He told His followers: "Blessed are you when men hate you, and when they exclude you, and revile you, and cast out your name as evil, for the Son of Man's sake. Rejoice in that day and leap for joy!" (Luke 6:22–23).

The writers of the epistles followed Jesus' lead:

- "You received the message with joy from the Holy Spirit in spite of the severe suffering it brought you" (1 Thessalonians 1:6 NLT).
- "My brethren, count it all joy when you fall into various trials" (James 1:2).

One of my favorite Bible stories is the story of Paul and Silas in the Philippian jail. They were beaten, they were imprisoned, and who knew what would happen to them the next day? "But at midnight Paul and Silas were praying and singing hymns to God, and the prisoners were listening to them" (Acts 16:25).

The kind of joy that gets you singing in jail at midnight with your back bleeding and your life hanging by a thread—that's joy worth cultivating!

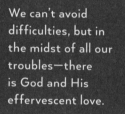

We can't avoid difficulties, but in the midst of all our troubles—there is God and His effervescent love.

In our culture of instant gratification and constant amusement, it's hard to understand the suffering the apostles endured for the sake of the gospel. We'll do anything to avoid trials and tribulations. But often, in an attempt to keep anything uncomfortable from touching us, we miss the very thing God wants to use to lead us to the joy in Him. We can't avoid difficulties, but in the midst of all our troubles—there is God and His effervescent love.

This doesn't mean we deny or disguise our feelings. It doesn't mean we can or should shrug off pain or disappointment or try not to feel sorrow when we have good cause. It means we place our trust in God, and He opens the door to a joy beyond anything we can know on our own: the joy of knowing we are in His hands forever.

THE JOY OF DEATH

Christian joy is so complete and lasting that it stays with us even when we are dying.

Tony Snow was one of America's most successful and respected newsmen and commentators. He rose from an op-ed writer and editor for a small newspaper to become a voice on ABC's *Good Morning America* and other network shows. His career took off when he moved to Fox News as host of his own show and was a frequent commentator on others. In 2006 President George W. Bush appointed Snow to be his White House press secretary. Though popular, knowledgeable, and highly articulate, he was forced to resign less than two years later when he was diagnosed with terminal colon cancer. He died the following year at fifty-three.

Tony Snow could have died a bitter man, angry at how his brilliant career was cut short at its peak and how cancer deprived him of life with his wife and three children. But Tony was a devout Christian. Far from being angry at God, he found joy in the unexpected blessing his illness brought him. He communicated this joy eloquently in an article published a few months before his death.

> God relishes surprise. We want lives of simple, predictable ease—smooth, even trails as far as the eye can see—but God likes to go off-road. He provokes us with twists and turns. He places us in predicaments that seem to defy our endurance and

What God
desires for
us, He also
provides
for us.

comprehension—and yet don't. By his love and grace, we persevere. The challenges that make our hearts leap and stomachs churn invariably strengthen our faith and grant measures of wisdom and joy we would not experience otherwise. . . .

The mere thought of death somehow makes every blessing vivid, every happiness more luminous and intense. We may not know how our contest with sickness will end, but we have felt the ineluctable touch of God.[3]

As Paul contemplated the conclusion of his life and ministry, he anticipated the joy that would be his at the end: "But none of these things move me; nor do I count my life dear to myself, so that I may finish my race with joy" (Acts 20:24). According to the apostle Peter, this joy is "inexpressible" (1 Peter 1:8). From his captivity on the isle of Patmos, John the apostle affirmed this dying joy: "Blessed are the dead who die in the Lord" (Revelation 14:13).

G. K. Chesterton believed this joy is "the gigantic secret of the Christian,"[4] and I believe he's right. Joy that thrives from the moment of our salvation to the moment of our death cannot be found outside of Christ! And what God desires for us, He also provides for us.

So don't settle for chasing happiness in this discouraging world. Even if you catch it, it won't last. Determine instead to accept and receive the gift of joy, and then watch in amazement as your life becomes a regular source of encouragement for everyone you encounter.

STUDY QUESTIONS

1. Read Proverbs 11:25. How does true biblical joy differ from the fleeting happiness sought after by so many of us?

....

....

....

....

....

....

....

....

....

....

2. How do people lose sight of the much greater
   joy to be found in Christ when they settle for
   momentary happiness?

....

....

....

....

....

....

....

....

....

....

....

....

3. Knowing that people often base their happiness on fleeting circumstances, behaviors, and attitudes, how much greater is it to have deep biblical joy that can be drawn on in any and all moments?

....

....

....

....

....

....

....

....

....

....

4. What has your personal experience been with the joys of salvation and baptism? If you've been baptized after accepting Christ, how can these initial steps toward Jesus encourage you as you continue to follow Him?

....

....

....

....

....

....

....

....

....

....

....

5. How can the story of Paul and Silas rejoicing in their prison cell motivate you to find joy in the midst of suffering?

....
....
....
....
....
....
....
....
....
....
....
....

6. Paul described his desire to finish his race "with joy." How can this attitude propel you forward as you seek to joyfully live out your days on earth before eternity in heaven?

....

....

....

....

....

....

....

....

....

....

....

Lord, I am immensely grateful for Your free gift of salvation. May I never move beyond gratitude for Your sacrifice on the cross, always keeping in perspective the perfect sacrifice that allowed me to first be made right with You and commune with You. Lead me, God, into greater and greater joy as I learn to trust in You. Let my life be a sacrifice to You in which I trade all my selfish plans for Your perfect plans, drawing joy from the eternal relationship with my Creator that I get to experience. Help me to seek lasting joy as I trust in You, casting aside the temporary happiness that is constantly tempting me to choose myself over You. As I move from the joys of salvation and baptism to the joys of trials and death, allow me to continue clinging to You and seeking You in all that I do. Let my life reflect the joy of Paul who sought to finish his race with joy, strengthening me to do the same. I pray this all with a humble confidence in Your strength and power to help me live as You have called me to live. Amen.

10

EVERLASTING

"Therefore, brethren, be even more diligent to make
your call and election sure, for if you do these things
you will never stumble; for so an entrance will be
supplied to you abundantly into the everlasting
kingdom of our Lord and Savior Jesus Christ."

2 PETER 1:10-11

C an you conceive of 860,300,000 words? That's how many
words the average person speaks in a lifetime.[1] Some people
are quieter, of course, while those who are more talkative can speak
more than a billion words. I may be one of them—I'm a preacher!

Now, imagine you've spoken 860,299,000 words and you
only have enough time for your last thousand. You know the end

of your life is very near, and every remaining phrase is precious. What would you want recorded for posterity?

Simon Peter's last message, the book of 2 Peter, is just over a thousand words in length. That's shorter than this chapter. I can envision him in the candlelight of his Roman cell, scratching out his final letter—the only way left for him to speak to the world. He weighed every word, considered every thought, and prayed over every sentence.

No wonder his epistle is so rich!

We started this book by reviewing 2 Peter 1:3 all the way back in chapter 1: "His divine power has given us everything we need for a godly life through our knowledge of him who called us by his own glory and goodness" (NIV). That's the first encouraging word we explored together: *everything*.

Now we're going to return to Peter's wonderful epistle and explore a second term, one that in many ways dwarfs everything else we've covered in these pages. That word is *everlasting*.

Let's take a look at that term in context:

> For if you possess these qualities in increasing measure, they will keep you from being ineffective and unproductive in your knowledge of our Lord Jesus Christ. But whoever does not have them is nearsighted and blind, forgetting that they have been cleansed from their past sins.
>
> Therefore, my brothers and sisters, make every effort to confirm your calling and election. For if you do these things, you will never stumble, and you will receive a rich welcome

into the eternal kingdom of our Lord and Savior Jesus Christ.
(2 Peter 1:8–11 NIV)

When Peter mentioned "these qualities," he was talking about eight essential character traits the Holy Spirit builds into our lives when we follow Christ: diligence, virtue, knowledge, self-control, perseverance, godliness, brotherly kindness, and love. When these virtues abound in our life, there's nothing we can't achieve for God's kingdom. We'll have everything we need for life and godliness.

But that's just the beginning! In verses 8–11 Peter listed seven distinct blessings God will pour out on those who follow Him—on those who pursue those eight qualities. We don't have time to explore all seven in these pages, so we'll focus on five in particular.

BLESSING ONE: GODLY MATURITY

The first blessing is the surge of godly maturity that accompanies your developing virtues.

After Peter listed his eight great qualities in verses 5–7, he wrote, "For if these things are yours and *abound*" (v. 8, emphasis added). Peter wanted early Christians to do more than have faith; he wanted them to devote themselves to growing deeper, wider, and richer in their faith. God wants the same for you—an abundant faith. Some of Peter's final recorded words were "grow in the grace and knowledge of our Lord and Savior Jesus Christ" (2 Peter 3:18).

God will work *through* you so you can be a blessing to others.

At times in Jesus' life, Peter seemed like the most immature disciple. But by the end of Peter's life, he had profound spiritual maturity and was ready to disclose the secret of how he had acquired it—through Jesus.

A word of caution: Don't confuse maturity with perfection. Qualities that lead to maturity are ever-expanding and ever-increasing; you'll never perfect them while you live on this earth. No matter how much knowledge you have, there's always more to tap into. No matter how much perseverance you develop, you can become even more resilient.

At the end of each year, I take a spiritual inventory of my life. I look back over the last twelve months and honestly evaluate my walk with Christ. There are always areas where I could have done better. But I can also track spiritual growth in my life. That growth is related to the development of character and virtue— "These things" I just mentioned. When I see that growth in my life, my confidence as a Christian is strengthened. I am Christ's, and He is mine. I am spiritually alive and becoming spiritually mature.

How are you doing in the maturity department? How mature is your faith, your joy, your patience, your wisdom in handling difficulties, your instincts for making wise decisions? What about your godliness, friendliness, and brotherly kindness?

If you're not where you'd like to be, don't be discouraged. Be diligent! Let these qualities abound in you. In the process, maturity happens.

And maturity is a thoroughly encouraging gift in our increasingly discouraging world.

BLESSING TWO: GROWING PRODUCTIVITY

Second Peter 1:8 goes on to say, "For if you possess these qualities in increasing measure, they will keep you from being ineffective and unproductive" (NIV). Peter put that in the negative, but let's restate it like this: "If you possess these eight qualities and grow in them, you'll be increasingly effective and productive in whatever you do for Christ."

Each of us has special gifts, talents, passions, opportunities, and assets for God's kingdom. Are you using your gifts effectively? Is God using you? I know of a man who used to pray, "Lord, use me!" Then it dawned on him to change his prayer to, "Lord, make me usable!"

That's what the virtues in 2 Peter do—they shape us into fruitful and effective servants for the kingdom. The key to productivity in Christian ministry is the diligent development of godly character in your life. As God works *in* you, developing you into a mature believer, He'll then work *through* you so you can be a blessing to others.

BLESSING THREE: GRATEFUL MEMORY

The next blessing that comes from abounding in the character traits God desires is a grateful memory. And once again, Peter used the negative to drive home the positive: "He who lacks these things is shortsighted, even to blindness, and has forgotten that he was cleansed from his old sins" (2 Peter 1:9).

Allow me to restate: If you grow in the qualities we've studied, you'll never forget how Christ has forgiven you of past sins. You'll keep Calvary in mind, always remembering how Jesus rescued, restored, and blessed you.

Peter warned against a complacent, satisfied faith. Instead, he wanted you to keep fresh in your memory the joy and thrill of your salvation. When you diligently seek to grow in Christlike character, you'll never lose the delight of what's happened to you.

As a young man, John Newton, who wrote the hymn "Amazing Grace," was involved in the evils of the slave trade. God saved him through the power of the blood of Christ, and Newton eventually became one of the greatest preachers and pastors of his age. He joined forces with England's abolitionists and saw the slave trade banned from the British Empire in 1807.

Near the end of his life, Newton received a visit from a friend, William Jay, who later wrote, "I saw Mr. Newton near the closing scene. He was hardly able to talk; and all I find I had noted down upon my leaving him was this: 'My memory is nearly gone, but I remember two things: That I am a great sinner and that Christ is a great Savior.'"[2]

Something I've noticed through years of reading the New Testament is the way the apostle Paul kept returning to the moment of his conversion on the Damascus road. He never forgot what God did for him that day. He never got over it.

You can get over a lot of things. You can get over loss and sadness and the problems that come with life, but you never want to get over Jesus or what He has done for you. As you grow in Him, your gratitude increases.

The best way to cultivate a grateful memory is to prompt yourself to be thankful. Always make it a point to say, "Thank You, Lord," throughout the day as He blesses you. Without His grace, your memory would be marred by regret, remorse, and shame. But through the blood of Christ, God has thrown all that behind His back. He's cast it as far as the east is from the west. We should never look back in anguish or embarrassment at anything in our lives, for God has washed away our sins. As we grow in Him, we grow in gratitude.

Let God heal your bad memories by enhancing your grateful recollections of His grace, and learn to be thankful to Him every day. He met you on your own Damascus road, He's washed away your guilt, He's cast your shame away, and He has given you a legacy of grace. Make sure you never get over it.

> Let God heal your bad memories by enhancing your grateful recollections of His grace, and learn to be thankful to Him every day.

BLESSING FOUR: GUARANTEED SECURITY

That brings us to the next blessing: guaranteed security. Notice how emphatically Peter put it in 2 Peter 1:10: "For if you do these things you will never stumble." Could Peter have been more emphatic in his statement? If you keep growing in these traits, you'll *never* stumble.

In other words, you'll never stumble on the highway to God's eternal home. You'll never tumble off the edge of the cliff and be lost. Peter didn't mean you'll never make a mistake or commit a sin. He meant you never have to worry about whether you're going to heaven. Your progress in the faith will serve as reassurance of your salvation.

J. D. Greear wrote that by age eighteen he'd probably asked Jesus into his heart five thousand times. One Saturday morning when he was four or five, he approached his parents asking about heaven. They explained the gospel message to him, and he asked Jesus to come into his life. His parents and his pastor felt it was a sincere decision, and they wrote the date in his Bible. "I lived in peace about the matter for nearly a decade," he said.

But in ninth grade he heard his Sunday school teacher say that many who think they're saved will awaken on the Judgment Day to hear Jesus say He never knew them. "I was terrified," wrote Greear. "Would I be one of those ones turned away?"

He asked Jesus to come into his heart again, this time with a resolve to be much more intentional about his faith. He was baptized again; but again, new doubts arose. He prayed the sinner's prayer again and again. "I walked a lot of aisles during those days," he wrote. "I think I've been saved at least once in every denomination."

In all, Greear was baptized four times! "Honestly, it got

pretty embarrassing. I became a staple at our church's baptism services. I got my own locker in the baptismal changing area."[3]

But here's the point: As Greear began growing in Christ and in the traits of godliness, his doubts and fears melted into faith and confidence. His growing maturity and stability led to growing confidence and security. Today he'll be glad to tell you how he knows without doubt that he's heaven bound.

If you have truly repented of your sins and trusted in the death and resurrection of Jesus Christ for salvation, you are saved! And as you grow in Jesus Christ, you will know you are saved. The very growth you experience in Christ will provide reassurance you've been born again.

Similarly, as you grow in the eight qualities Peter described, you won't stumble into doubting your salvation because you'll be drawing from His divine power and standing on His precious promises. His very personality will surge through you to create the qualities that give stability and security to life.

> If you have truly repented of your sins and trusted in the death and resurrection of Jesus Christ for salvation, you are saved!

I can tell you from experience, the blessing of security is invaluable as an anchor of encouragement in a sea of trouble.

BLESSING FIVE: GLORIOUS ETERNITY

That leads us to the final blessing—a glorious eternity! Follow Peter's logic in 2 Peter 1:10–11 as he brought the paragraph to a thrilling climax: "Therefore, brethren, be even more diligent to make your call and election sure, for if you do these things you will never stumble; for so an entrance will be supplied to you abundantly into the everlasting kingdom of our Lord and Savior Jesus Christ."

Peter wasn't suggesting we get into the Lord's kingdom by building character in our lives. We can't work our way into heaven on our own merits or by our own efforts. Instead, he was saying that if we diligently add these spiritual qualities to our Christian lives, we'll be given a rich, or an abundant, entrance into eternity.

Take a moment to think about that word: *everlasting*. As in the blessings we receive from Christ will last forever. The life we get to live through Christ will last forever. There will be no end to God's "everlasting kingdom."

What could be more encouraging than the promise of eternal life? And not just life—not just being biologically alive—but eternal peace, purpose, and joy in the presence of the living God.

There is no greater gift we could receive.

In my book *Living with Confidence in a Chaotic World*, I compared heaven to a safe and pleasant harbor. Throughout our lives, we sail godward toward that harbor, moving through the storms and the rocks that lurk in the waves. Some ships barely make it into port. The crew is exhausted and near mutiny, the sails are torn, supplies are low, and the ship has sprung many leaks. It's not exactly a hail-the-conquering-hero kind of arrival.

But we don't have to float into harbor with our sails down and our spirits defeated. Peter was telling us that diligent believers are like attentive captains and sailors; they sail with discipline, manning the watchtower, maintaining the ship, keeping morale high among the crew. Storms will come, but God has given us what we need to come through each one stronger.[4]

Yes, there are storms ahead. Yes, we will endure much sorrow and difficulty as we navigate this discouraging world filled with disappointments, dejection, and despair.

Yet we are not alone. We have the presence of God's Spirit to guide us. We have the power of God's Word to inspire us. And we have the people of God's kingdom to come alongside us no matter what we may face.

Therefore, take heart. Choose to be encouraged by these ten truths from God's Word, and choose to live as a source of encouragement for others!

STUDY QUESTIONS

1. Read 2 Peter 1:10–11. What qualities does Peter list to receive a rich welcome into the everlasting kingdom of heaven?

....

....

....

....

....

....

....

....

....

2. How does focusing on the everlasting things of heaven propel us beyond the short-sightedness of the things of today?

....

....

....

....

....

....

....

....

....

....

....

....

3. God promises throughout Scripture to work
   both in us and through us. How does this
   overflow of God's work in our lives to others
   around us magnify the importance of a personal
   relationship with Him?

....

....

....

....

....

....

....

....

....

....

4. What can we do now to better prepare ourselves to bless others in the future?

....

....

....

....

....

....

....

....

....

....

....

....

5. We are reminded of the presence of God's Spirit, the power of God's Word, and the people of God's kingdom as anchors to keep us aligned with God's mission for us on this earth. How can we lean into these blessings and have an eternal mindset?

....

....

....

....

....

....

....

....

....

....

6. What has the Lord been teaching you during this time of learning, and how will it affect your future relationship with the Lord? How has it been an encouragement in the midst of discouraging times?

....

....

....

....

....

....

....

....

....

....

Father, I am reminded of Your holiness and my inadequacy in comparison. It drives me to be that much more grateful for all that You have blessed me with. Help me to have an eternal perspective that allows me to look beyond the temporary things of today that seem to loom so large. Guide me in the pursuit of godly maturity as I follow You, and remind me of Your continued goodness and faithfulness all along the way. I admit that I have often fallen into the trap of forgetting my eternal blessings in discouraging moments, and I ask for Your encouragement to buoy me into the next phase of Your will for my life. Let me be a model of an imperfect person humbly seeking the perfection of Christ in His attitudes and actions. Lead me in Your righteousness, and help me to fend off the crippling discouragement of this world by clinging closer and closer to You. Restore the joy of Your salvation to me, and sustain me by giving me a willing spirit. I pray this all to Your glory. Amen.

NOTES

CHAPTER 1: EVERYTHING

1. "Gifts for Person Who Has Everything," Amazon.com (accessed April 13, 2023), https://www.amazon.com/s?k=gifts+for+person+who+has+everything&hvadid=570569766866&hvdev=c&hvlocphy=9012334&hvnetw=g&hvqmt=e&hvrand=17280262472670300582&hvtargid=kwd-5721545084&hydadcr=13993_13379046&tag=googhydr-20&ref=pd_sl_ar2kf9phy_e.

2. Everek R. Storms, "Standing on the Promises," *Contact Magazine*, March, 1978, 13–14.

3. Adapted and used with permission from Robert J. Morgan, *All to Jesus: A Year of Devotions* (Nashville, TN: B&H Publishing Group, 2012), Day 168.

CHAPTER 2: SUFFICIENT

1. Gordon MacDonald, *The Life God Blesses* (Nashville, TN: Thomas Nelson, 1994), 25.

2. Charles Stanley, *How to Handle Adversity* (Nashville, TN: Thomas Nelson, 1991), 117.

CHAPTER 3: BOUNTIFULLY

1. Alex Stone, "Why Waiting Is Torture," *New York Times*, August 18, 2012, https://www.nytimes.com/2012/08/19/opinion/sunday/why-waiting-in-line-is-torture.html.
2. Tom Petty, "The Waiting," Produced by Tom Petty and Jimmy Iovine, recorded by Tom Petty and the Heartbreakers, released on *Hard Promises*, Backstreet Records, (c)1981.

CHAPTER 4: REFUGE

1. "The full story of Thailand's extraordinary cave rescue," BBC News, July 14, 2018, https://www.bbc.com/news/world-asia-44791998.
2. Alexander MacLaren, *The Psalms*, vol. 3, *Psalms 90–150* (New York: A. C. Armstrong & Son, 1894), 408.

CHAPTER 5: MIGHT

1. Denny Morrison, "Denny Frank on Cheating Death Twice to Make It Back to the Olympics," *Vice Sports*, January 23, 2018, https://sports.vice.com/en_ca/article/mbpdg8/denny-morrison-on-cheating-death-twice-to-make-it-back-to-the-olympics.
2. Robert J. Morgan, *Nelson's Complete Book of Stories, Illustrations, and Quotes* (Nashville, TN: Thomas Nelson, 2000), 64–65.

CHAPTER 6: PEACE

1. Joe Martin, "Ex-Energy Employee Smashes into New Career Path," *Houston Business Journal*, May 31, 2016, https://www.bizjournals.com /houston/news/2016/05/31/ex-energy-employee-smashes-into-new-career-path.html.
2. "Facts and Statistics," Anxiety and Depression Association of America, accessed April 17, 2018, https://adaa.org/about-adaa/press-room/facts-statistics.

3. Joseph Stromberg, "7 Things the Most-Highlighted Kindle Passages Tell Us about American Readers," Vox, June 8, 2014, https:// www.vox.com/2014/6/8/5786196/7-things-the-most-highlighted-kindle-passages-tell-us-about-american.
4. See entry for "Merimnao" at *Bible Hub*, accessed May 16, 2018, http://biblehub.com/greek/3309.htm.
5. Kim Phuc Phan Thi, "These Bombs Led Me to Christ," *Christianity Today*, April 20, 2018, https://www.christianitytoday.com/ct/2018/may/napalm-girl-kim-phuc-phan-thi-fire-road.html.

CHAPTER 7: WISDOM

1. Sinclair Ferguson, *Grow in Grace* (Colorado Springs, CO: NavPress, 1984), 236–37.
2. Tremper Longman III, *Baker Commentary on the Old Testament and Psalms: Proverbs* (Grand Rapids, MI: Baker Academic, 2006), 101.
3. Thomas Jefferson, *The Writings of Thomas Jefferson, Volume 17* (Washington, DC: The Thomas Jefferson Memorial Association, 1905), 130.
4. A. W. Tozer, *The Pursuit of God* (Harrisburg, PA: Christian Pub. Co., 1948), 17.
5. Lady Julian of Norwich, *Revelations of Divine Love* (London: Methuen, 1911), 12.
6. John Meacham, *American Gospel: God, the Founding Fathers, and the Making of a Nation* (New York, NY: Random House, 2007), 173.

CHAPTER 8: COMPASSION

1. Adapted from David Jeremiah, *Living with Confidence in a Chaotic World* (Nashville, TN: Thomas Nelson, 2009), 39.

CHAPTER 9: JOY

1. Edward K. Rowell, ed., *1001 Quotes, Illustrations, and Humorous Stories for Preachers, Teachers, and Writers* (Grand Rapids, MI: Baker Books, 2008), 177, 220.

2. J. P. Moreland and Klaus Issler, *The Lost Virtue of Happiness* (Colorado Springs, CO: NavPress, 2006), 14–15.

3. Tony Snow, "Cancer's Unexpected Blessings," *Christianity Today*, July 20, 2007, http://www.christianitytoday.com/ct/2007/july/25.30.html.

4. G. K. Chesterton, *Orthodoxy* (New York: John Lane, 1909), 298.

CHAPTER 10: EVERLASTING

1. Gyles Brandreth, *The Joy of Lex: How to Have Fun with 860,341,500 Words* (New York, NY: William Morrow & Co., 1983).

2. Jonathan Aitken, *John Newton* (Wheaton, IL: Crossway Books, 2007), 347.

3. J. D. Greear, *Stop Asking Jesus into Your Heart: How to Know for Sure You Are Saved* (Nashville, TN: B&H Publishing, 2013), 2–3.

4. David Jeremiah, *Living with Confidence in a Chaotic World* (Nashville, TN: Thomas Nelson, 2009), 87.

ABOUT THE AUTHOR

D r. David Jeremiah is the founder of Turning Point, an international ministry committed to providing Christians with sound Bible teaching through radio and television, the Internet, live events, and resource materials and books. He is the author of more than seventy-five books, including *Forward*, *Where Do We Go From Here?*, and *The Book of Signs*.

Dr. Jeremiah serves as the senior pastor of Shadow Mountain Community Church in El Cajon, California. He and his wife, Donna, have four children and twelve grandchildren.